THE ECONOMICS OF NEIGHBORLY L♥VE

INVESTING IN YOUR COMMUNITY'S COMPASSION AND CAPACITY

TOM NELSON

IVP Books

An imprint of InterVarsity Press
Downers Grove, Illinois

InterVarsity Press
P.O. Box 1400, Downers Grove, IL 60515-1426
ivpress.com
email@ivpress.com

*InterVarsity Press® is the book-publishing division of InterVarsity Christian Fellowship/USA®, a
movement of students and faculty active on campus at hundreds of universities, colleges, and schools
of nursing in the United States of America, and a member movement of the International Fellowship
of Evangelical Students. For information about local and regional activities, visit intervarsity.org.*

Cover design: Faceout Studio
Interior design: Jeanna Wiggins
Images: wooded road background: © Piotr Zajada/Shutterstock
*   dollar bill: custom photo by Derek Thornton/Faceout Studio*

ISBN 978-0-8308-4392-3 (print)
ISBN 978-0-8308-8932-7 (digital)

Printed in the United States of America ♾

Library of Congress Cataloging-in-Publication Data

A catalog record for this book is available from the Library of Congress.

P 25 24 23 22 21 20 19 18 17 16 15 14 13 12 11 10 9 8 7 6 5 4 3 2 1

Y 34 33 32 31 30 29 28 27 26 25 24 23 22 21 20 19 18 17

"With characteristic winsomeness and clarity, Nelson covers a wide range of topics from poverty to jobs and justice to entrepreneurship, providing a highly readable overview of biblically informed economic life. This pastor has taken the time to learn about the capacity that makes genuine compassion possible. Implicit in the book is a much-needed correction to the church: we've far too long avoided the work of thinking well about economics, as though somehow that sphere is detached from our spiritual life. Nelson shows us the Bible talks about economics through and through—it's just that too many pastors haven't been paying sufficient attention. Nelson has given us an accessible introductory textbook for understanding what makes for flourishing people and communities."

Amy L. Sherman, author of *Kingdom Calling: Vocational Stewardship for the Common Good*

"For several years I've watched this book being born, growing out of Tom Nelson's remarkable work as a pastor in Kansas City and increasingly as a teacher to the wider world. *The Economics of Neighborly Love* makes this simple argument: the everyday world is an economic world, and there are implications for who we are and how we live. Drawing on years of pastoral experience with people at work in the world, social analysis from across the political spectrum, relationships with good people doing good work in cities all over America, and, most profoundly, a commitment to biblical and theological reflection, this is a book for everyone who cares about the moral meaning of the marketplace."

Steven Garber, principal of the Washington Institute for Faith, Vocation & Culture, author of *Visions of Vocation*

"This desperately needed book shows that a concern for fruitfulness—relational and vocational—is a deep pattern running through Scripture, literally from beginning to end. Fruitfulness in all our work and relationships is essential to discipleship to Jesus Christ, which is at the heart of the identity and mission of God's people. Tom Nelson has done both the church and the world an extraordinary service by giving it the fruitful gift of this book."

Greg Forster, Trinity International University

"I don't think I've ever seen the words 'economics' and 'neighborly love' in the same sentence. With winsome intelligence and a natural storyteller's gift, Tom Nelson reminds us that faith, economics, and work—rightly understood—help create the conditions for neighborly love to exist and flourish."

David W. Miller, director, Princeton University Faith & Work Initiative, president, the Avodah Institute

"It's hard to imagine a book that is more urgently needed in our time of history. And it's hard to imagine a more incisive, compassionate, biblical, and relevant discussion of economics and Christian faith. Nelson combines scriptural wisdom, cultural awareness, pastoral sensitivity, and practical expression to guide us into a deeper understanding of how our faith must be lived in the complex realm of economics. . . . *The Economics of Neighborly Love* holds together what we have so often and so wrongly put asunder: faithfulness and flourishing, productivity and justice, compassion and creativity, wealth and love. The result is a book that should be read by pastors and church leaders, to be sure, but also by all followers of Jesus who seek to live faithful and fruitful lives in today's world."

Mark D. Roberts, executive director, Max De Pree Center for Leadership

"Tom Nelson's new book is a great contribution to a growing and needed literature that helps churches connect to their parishes and neighborhoods and serve not only individuals, but the public good. There is an emerging awareness of the importance of this, but few volumes are as practical as this one in describing the way forward. I recommend it!"

Tim Keller, Redeemer Presbyterian Church, New York City

"Money, spirituality, and responsibility are rarely put together side by side in a balanced way. *The Economics of Neighborly Love* takes you there in a way that will encourage the practical understanding and development of resources, leading to flourishing. I highly commend this book."

Darrell Bock, senior research professor of New Testament studies, executive director for cultural engagement, Dallas Theological Seminary

"I'm delighted to see this insightful book by Tom Nelson hit the streets! Tom connects work and economics with theological skill, biblical acumen, and a pastoral heart. He rightly sees how economics is intimately connected to our ability to flourish as human beings, our mandate to be productive in the world, and our obligation to love our neighbors. When reading this book, you will feel as if you're sitting down with Tom over a cup of coffee for a conversation about some of life's most important matters, and thankfully you don't have to be an expert in economics to follow the conversation. Tom is a great guide through this material, since it comes out of his lived experience, both personally and as a longtime pastor. This is a book about why economics matters—how personal compassion and economic capacity both are important."

Scott B. Rae, dean of faculty, professor of Christian ethics, Talbot School of Theology, Biola University, La Mirada, California

"I have many books on Christianity and economics in my library. Tom Nelson's *The Economics of Neighborly Love* will be shelved among the best. It represents an optimal combination of solid theology, sound economics, and specific applications. If you've already read Sider, Corbett, and Fikkert, Nelson's book will be a valuable complement. If you've not yet read them, start with Nelson. You will be challenged, instructed, and edified. Not many books on economics can pull off this hat trick."

Kenneth G. Elzinga, Robert C. Taylor Professor of Economics, University of Virginia

"There is no secular/spiritual divide. Every Jesus-follower who labors in the marketplace has a ministry just as significant as those who labor in the pulpit. In *The Economics of Neighborly Love*, Tom Nelson points the way to a genuine biblical worldview that grasps the powerful spiritual interconnectedness between what happens in the marketplace, our churches, communities, nation, world, and our walk with Jesus. I highly recommend it."

Larry Osborne, author, pastor, North Coast Church, Vista, California

"Tom Nelson thoughtfully and carefully weaves together biblical truth, deep theological reflection, and sound economic thinking in *The Economics of Neighborly Love*. It fills a significant void in economic and biblical writing. Too often economic essays ignore biblical wisdom while theological reflections on human flourishing pay little attention to the potential of economic activity, especially the opportunity for people to serve others through marketplace endeavors. Nelson avoids both problems and has written a superb book that will be valuable to pastors, seminary professors, and people in the work place."

P. J. Hill, professor emeritus of economics, Wheaton College

"Pastor Tom Nelson has written an important book for our turbulent times. With communities and congregations beset by conflict and political polarization, this focus on economic flourishing rooted in personal wholeness offers biblical hope and practical wisdom for discipleship and mission. Connecting the divine design of Genesis 1–2 with the destiny of Revelation 21–22, Nelson argues for a hopeful realism rooted in the present activity of the Holy Spirit in and through the local church. Pastors will find this work helpful as they connect Sunday worship with Monday work, deep spiritual intimacy with economic integrity, and ecstatic experiences with ethical transformation."

Charlie Self, professor of church history, The Assemblies of God Theological Seminary, director of city development, Made to Flourish, author of *Flourishing Churches and Communities*

"There is no one writing today more adept at seeing the practical intersections of economics, theology, and the Christian faith than Tom Nelson. There is also no one better positioned to encourage Christians to live inside the biblical narrative by thinking theologically and engaging economically. From these angles, Nelson shows us that creating economic capacity is inextricably connected to the call of the gospel to look beyond ourselves toward the care of our neighbors as the best means of our own flourishing. Creating economic capacity for the sake of compassion is the heart of Nelson's plea. It's a plea that desperately needs to be heard inside churches and inside the hearts of Christians across the globe. We are in Nelson's debt for making that plea so clearly and powerfully."

Richard Lints, Andrew Mutch Distinguished Professor of Theology, vice president for academic affairs, Gordon-Conwell Theological Seminary

"In *The Economics of Neighborly Love*, Tom Nelson has given the church a powerful gift. He masterfully holds in tension the beauty of God's economic design with the realities of economic brokenness in our world. In my role, I regularly see the 'already' and the 'not yet' of God's design in action. I pray that Tom's clarion call to love what God loves, to embrace his design for generosity and human flourishing while working toward the alleviation of economic injustice, is not only heard but put into practice. Tom, thanks for this remarkable gift. "

Jonathan Rich, major, metroplex commander, The Salvation Army

"Tom Nelson is one of the best thinkers and one of the most accessible writers in the faith-and-work movement. His storytelling is unmatched in the way he is able to both capture the imagination and convey a solid truth. In *The Economics of Neighborly Love*, he doesn't just teach a theology of economics, he also invites us to love our neighbors through our everyday work. Pastors and laypersons will find practical and rich treasures within these pages."

Bethany Jenkins, director, Every Square Inch

THIS BOOK IS DEDICATED TO

Robert and Patricia Kern, and their daughter Marcia.

*I am most grateful for their well-lived lives
and for the philanthropic legacy of
neighborly love they embody.*

CONTENTS

INTRODUCTION

We don't *like* nuts on our cake!"
Those were the deceptive words my mother blurted out to a
fellow elementary student in a rural Wisconsin schoolhouse during
the era of the Great Depression. Her more materially advantaged
school chum simply couldn't fathom why the cake in my mom's
lunch pail didn't have sugary frosting with nuts on top. A shy and
sensitive young girl, my mom immediately felt the shame of her
family's material impoverishment. Mom had not taken an economics class, but even so, she intuitively knew economic realities
mattered in everyday life.

Nuts on a cake were a luxury her family could not afford.

As mom recounted this moment years later to her seven awe-
struck children, she made clear that outright deception seemed to
be her only option at the time. How else could she protect her
proper sense of human dignity? Lying was not habit for her. But I
find it telling that this boldface lie came out quickly and easily when
an insensitive schoolmate backed her into an economic corner.

Like my mom, I too grew up in rural poverty. My father's un-
timely death amplified the number of times my six siblings and I
faced the struggle of material impoverishment. On more than one
occasion we felt the shame of our own "we don't like nuts on our
cake" moments. During our daily bus rides home from school, our
family poverty could not be masked. Schoolmates would ask, "When

are you going to paint your house?" Following our mother's example, we too lied through our teeth, offering up plausible yet deceptive reasons for the glaringly neglected appearance of our home.

Even as a ten-year-old boy, I knew house paint was a luxury far beyond our single mother's meager budget. Although I had little economic understanding at the time, I could see that the world I'd been born into was an economic one, and that the economics of a family mattered. Though she never spoke a single complaining word, I was aware it was a herculean struggle for my mom to make sure we had enough food on the table. The exterior of the house would have to wait. There were more pressing matters at hand. The bus ride home would remain a regular and unwelcome reminder that we were poor—a reminder that often prompted me to question my own worth and value.

One of the most painful memories from my early adolescence occurred after a softball game with a few friends. I found myself at a drive-in restaurant where I realized I could not afford a single item on the menu. Suddenly I wasn't hungry anymore. I fought back tears while I stood beside my teammates. And when I got home that night, I drenched my pillow in a flood of sorrow.

Though I had not yet taken an economics class or even thought about supply and demand; though I hadn't heard the names of Milton Friedman, Friedrich Hayek, and John Maynard Keynes, I knew in the depths of my heart that economics mattered, and mattered a lot. I couldn't articulate it at the time, but I began to grasp on a personal level that economic flourishing and human flourishing were intricately connected.

Yet even as our family was materially impoverished, we experienced spiritual richness through our Christian faith and in our local church. But growing up I was puzzled as to why so many in our church didn't seem to care about our family's economic stresses and vulnerabilities. Was it a lack of compassion? A lack of capacity? Or was it something different altogether? As a single parent, my mom worked extraordinarily hard at a relatively low-paying job. The economic challenges we faced were not hard for others to see. Indeed, material poverty not only weighs on the human heart but also on the sleeves. I'm sure our economic situation was apparent to those around us. Nevertheless, the Christian faith of our local church felt deeply disconnected from the economic challenges we experienced. Each day, I woke up in an economic world, yet the Christian faith I was taught seemed to have little to say about it. I wondered why this was: Did Christian faith have anything to do with the economic world I lived, worked, and played in?

As a young adult this important question was put on the back burner for a time, even as I pursued a college degree in business. I took classes in macroeconomics, microeconomics, and economic statistics. I learned about classical and modern economics. I was exposed to Adam Smith, as well as the Austrian, Keynesian, and Chicago Schools of economic thought. Even so, my painful childhood experiences and the deep disconnect I experienced between my Christian faith and my economic life laid fallow in the recesses of my mind and my heart.

A few years later, I sensed God's call to serve the local church in a pastoral role. That meant seminary education and theological study. Yet again, the question of how Christian faith might speak into economic life was sidestepped, as the worlds of theology and everyday work were presented to me as entirely separate spheres, which were kept planets apart in my seminary classrooms.

In my professional education for pastoral ministry, I do not recall any serious discussion about economics or its connection to faith or to the local church. As an impressionable seminarian this neglect further reinforced a dualistic understanding of the world, deepening the faulty notion that pastoral work and economic life had little in common. Economics was for economists; theology was for pastors. There were no points of intersection—or so I believed.

It wasn't until I'd served for a few years in pastoral ministry that the burning questions of my childhood revisited me. How did Christian faith speak meaningfully to everyday life? What did it have to say about work and economics? I needed answers. After an extensive reexamination of the biblical text and a careful revisiting of the writings of the Protestant Reformers, I came to a sobering conclusion. Due to an impoverished understanding of Scripture, I had been perpetuating an improperly dualistic Sunday-to-Monday gap through my teaching and ministry. Wrongly, I had separated the life of Christian faith from ordinary, everyday living in the world. Though I had experienced economic hardship, and though I had studied economic theory and Christian theology, I had failed to connect faith and economics in a meaningful way.

This was an inconvenient truth as a young pastor. I had made a grave mistake. Operating out of an impoverished biblical theology and pastoral paradigm, I had been spending the majority of my time equipping the congregation I served for the minority of their lives. I had to call it what it was: malpractice. This pastoral malpractice was impoverishing our congregation in its spiritual formation and gospel mission. To be faithful in my vocational calling, I knew deep in my bones that this massive gap needed to dramatically narrow.

By God's grace over the past twenty years, the Sunday-to-Monday gap is beginning to shrink in the parish I serve, though we still have miles to go. In my conversations with other pastors and Christian leaders, I've come to see that my story of pastoral malpractice is not unique. It is tragically common. I now realize the gap is far bigger and more perilous than I first imagined. The rightful worship of God, the spiritual formation of God's people, the plausibility and proclamation of the gospel, and the common good of our neighbors—both local and global—are crippled because we have long neglected to rightly understand how the gospel speaks to every nook and cranny of life, including our work and economic systems. Pastors and Christian leaders in all vocations are called to care for the vulnerable and to seek the flourishing of every image bearer of God. I hope this work will contribute to that high and holy task.

I am delighted that so many have recently written on the deep and significant connections between faith and work, making the case that our individual work truly matters to God and to our neighbors. Yet, while our personal vocations do, of course, matter a great deal, they are by no means the entire story. Our work always takes place within larger economic realities; we are part of a much bigger story. All of our collaborative, value-adding work takes place within a system of cooperative global exchange. This is what modern, everyday economics is all about. From my pastoral perspective, far too little has been written or taught to the rising generation of leaders about how theology and economics seamlessly intersect. The glaring irony is that Holy Scripture speaks a good deal about economic flourishing. Yet in our personal lives, in our congregations, and in our work, we all too often woefully neglect to connect the gospel of the kingdom with economics. This harms our witness, our cities, and our future. The church needs to address and begin the hard work of overcoming the perilous Sunday-to-Monday gap.

Does Christian faith have anything to do with the economic world we live, work, and play in? As a young boy growing up in a materially impoverished, single-parent home, I wrestled with that question. Today, I am still wrestling, even as I've begun to ask other questions as well: What does the Bible say about economics? What does a life of fruitfulness look like? What role do Christian leaders have in nurturing the economic well-being of their congregations and organizations? What about the economic well-being of the cities where they minister and serve?

From this crucible of my own pastoral malpractice, and in the gracious providence of God, I am hopeful that some of the insights I have assembled in the pages that follow will stretch your mind, inspire your heart, and spark your imagination in new ways. My prayer is that you might become more like Jesus, better loving your neighbor, and growing in fruitfulness to your vocational calling within the larger web of economic order that the God of history has marvelously invited us to inhabit.

1

NEIGHBORLY LOVE

It is a serious thing to live in a society of possible gods and goddesses, to remember that the dullest most uninteresting person you can talk to may one day be a creature which, if you saw it now, you would be strongly tempted to worship, or else a horror and a corruption such as you now meet, if at all, only in a nightmare. It is in light of these overwhelming possibilities, it is with awe and the circumspection proper to them, that we should conduct our dealings with one another, all friendships, all loves, all play, all politics. There are no ordinary people. You have never talked to a mere mortal. Nations, cultures, arts, civilizations—these are mortal, and their life is to ours as the life of a gnat. But it is immortals whom we joke with, work with, marry, snub and exploit—immortal horrors or everlasting splendors. Next to the Blessed Sacrament itself, your neighbor is the holiest object presented to your senses.

C. S. LEWIS, "THE WEIGHT OF GLORY"

You shall love the Lord your God with all your heart and with all your soul and with all your strength and with all your mind, and your neighbor as yourself.

LUKE 10:27

O n a plane from Portland to Kansas City, I sat by two young men who were on their way to visit their retired father, now living in Arkansas. As we chatted in casual conversation, the younger brother informed me he had graduated from a highly reputable college two years prior. Like the sword of Damocles, the burden of sizeable college loans precariously dangled over his financial future. Though he had been searching job listings on a number of websites, he hadn't been able to find an adequately paying job that would allow him to cover his rent and to begin paying off his student loans. With a fearful glisten in his eyes he looked at me, someone who had been a total stranger only moments earlier, and transparently said, "It's really hard out there. I am not sure what I am going to do." Hearing the cry of his heart, my attempt to offer some encouraging words seemed hollow at best.

As a young boy I remember hearing the blaring heart cry of a restless generation echoing from my oldest brother's high-powered stereo. The words of pop singer Jackie DeShannon still ring in my ears with crystal clarity. "What the world needs now is love, sweet love, / it's the only thing there is just too little of." The world still needs lots of love, but the heart cry I hear from so many today is "what the world needs now is jobs, sweet jobs, it's the only thing there is just too little of."

In my pastoral vocation the most frequent conversations I have with congregants do not revolve around their troubling spiritual or existential questions, or even their relational problems and difficulties, but rather focus on their many economic challenges. The parents of a high school student approaching her senior year tell me they are anxious about helping their child handle the high expense of a college education. They want their daughter to go to college, but they don't want her saddled with loads of debt. What are they to do? As a pastor, how am I to respond to the cry of their anxious hearts? Following a Sunday morning worship service, a senior citizen confides in me her need for pastoral prayer. I ask how I can pray for her, anticipating she desires that I pray for her health or the well-being of her grandchildren. But she is concerned by historic low interest rates, and the consequently meager return she receives on her savings. She's worried about outliving her financial resources and becoming a financial burden to her children. What do I say? How do I pray?

The everyday world we live in is an economic world. Daily we are confronted with global economic realities that impact us in a myriad of stress-filled ways. We may lose our job to downsizing. We may face unemployment or underemployment. Job reports and housing stats immediately affect the financial markets, consumer confidence, and our retirement accounts. An unwelcome rush of worry ambushes us with the alarming economic headlines.

Additionally, the growing challenges of cyber security and the rapid pace of technological advance are profoundly reshaping the very nature of work itself. In an article titled "A World Without Work," Derek Thompson makes the case that technological change, particularly the development of increasingly complex and skilled robots, will "exert a slow but continual downward pressure on the value and availability of work—that is on wages and on the share of prime-age workers with full-time jobs."[1] Taking a different view is economic historian Joel Mokyr, who argues that though jobs will dramatically change in terms of skills needed, there still will be meaningful work to do in the future.[2]

Regardless of how the future unfolds, numerous challenges, pressures, and questions loom on the economic horizon of our ever-changing globalized economy. What will work look like in the future? How will changing demographics impact the job market? Will there be enough workers? Or too many? And where will new jobs come from?

The heartfelt concern I hear from so many people is not merely, Does my work matter? but also, Is there meaningful work for me to do? They wonder if they will be able to earn a decent living to pay their bills. They worry about whether they will have enough money in their retirement. The human need for security never ends. And our rapidly changing economic world makes it difficult to respond to these sincere concerns with confidence.

THE GREAT COMMANDMENT

Our world is asking serious questions. And as followers of Jesus, we have little to say in response. As gospel people we affirm that integral, biblical faith speaks into every nook and cranny of life. But many times our Christian faith has not informed our thinking, our prayers, and our priorities when it comes to our global economy and the economic opportunity of others. Our lack of thoughtful engagement in the economic challenges of our world is in part due to an impoverished understanding of Jesus' teaching on the Great Commandment. Could it be we are overlooking something very important?

Jesus taught that loving God and our neighbor is at the very heart of Christian faith, but what does loving our neighbor look like in daily life? Is it about taking soup to our neighbor when they are sick or mowing our neighbor's lawn when they are on vacation? Is it about inviting our neighbors to dinner or to church? Of course these tangible gestures of love are good and right for the apprentice of Jesus, but a careful study of Jesus' teaching suggests he had more in mind when he spoke about neighborly love. Jesus teaches us that neighborly love speaks into the collaborative work we do every day. He insists that our neighborly love should fuel economic flourishing. Understanding this teaching is vital, particularly in our increasingly global and interconnected world.

A closer look at the New Testament Gospels reveals that Jesus talked more about money, work, and economics than we might at first imagine. Most of Jesus' parables were closely tied to the agrarian economy of the first century. Klaus Issler notes, "Of the thirty-seven parables in the Synoptic Gospels, thirty-two mention some form of work-related activity as part of the storyline."[3] Understanding Jesus' economic interest and competency should not be surprising when we remember that Jesus spent the majority of his life on earth learning carpentry and running a small business. In Jesus' first-century context, he was known first and foremost as a carpenter from Nazareth.[4]

When Jesus became an itinerant rabbi, he often preached in marketplaces, surrounded by buyers and sellers. What if brilliant Jesus was truly an insightful economist? What if Jesus points us to the economics textbook we had in high school or college? What if the Bible has a great deal to say about economic flourishing?

In Luke 10, we encounter a compelling narrative that gives us profound insight into the economics of neighborly love. Jesus engages in conversation with a legal expert who was highly trained in Old Testament law. The lawyer asks Jesus how one inherits eternal life, and Jesus responds with a question: What does the Old Testament have to say about that? The legal expert responds to Jesus with what has come to be known as The Great Commandment: "You shall love the Lord your God with all your heart and with all your soul and with all your strength and with all your mind, and your neighbor as yourself" (Lk 10:27). After affirming the lawyer's wise insight, extracted from two Old Testament texts (Deut 6:5; Lev 19:18), Jesus instructs the lawyer to embody this reality, bringing it to bear on all aspects of his everyday life. It certainly seems like Jesus' assertion will put an end to the conversation, but the discussion continues.

In the exchange that follows, Luke provides an insightful glimpse into the true intent motivating the lawyer's question. It becomes clear that this Old Testament expert is more interested in trying to discredit Jesus than he is in learning from Jesus. The heart of the lawyer's problem is his heart. The lawyer is most interested in earning his way into God's acceptance and love. By recording the lawyer's follow-up question, "Who is my neighbor?" Luke allows us to observe the massive gap between what the lawyer knew was right and how he actually lived out the Old Testament mandate to love God and his neighbor. In asking this question, the lawyer betrays that he's looking for loopholes.

Rather than giving a pat answer, Jesus tells a riveting story that not only addresses the question "Who is my neighbor?" but also reveals insight into another important question: What does loving our neighbor require? Jesus speaks of a man who was making the arduous seventeen-mile trek from Jerusalem to Jericho. Along the way this man, who likely was Jewish, becomes a victim of thugs who rob him, beat him, and leave him for dead. In the aftermath, a Jewish priest traveling the same road stumbles on the beaten man. But he keeps walking. Although we are curious, Jesus doesn't tell us what this Jewish religious leader is thinking. Perhaps in his heart and mind an intense tug of war ensues. Should he maintain ritual purity by avoiding contact with blood or seek to aid the needy stranger, who is badly wounded and might already be dead? The ethical deliberating doesn't last long. The Jewish priest keeps his pace, leaving a very needy and desperate stranger lying on the side of the road, woefully vulnerable and unattended.

But not all hope is lost. A glimmer of promise enters the story as another religious leader, a Jewish Levite, comes down the same road. For whatever reason, the Levite also passes by. Just like the priest, he walks past the man without offering help or assistance.

Things are looking increasingly grim until a Samaritan comes down the road. Culturally, it is likely the Samaritan was not a religious leader but rather a person seeking to engage in a business transaction in Jericho. Strategically located on routes of trade, Jericho was a center of commerce and economic activity in the first century. It is important to realize that both racially and religiously, Jews looked down on Samaritans. Yet in Jesus' story, the Samaritan crosses formidable barriers of human indifference, racial bigotry, and religious prejudice to offer aid to the gravely beaten Jewish man. But even more, the Samaritan interrupts his business trip to take the desperately needy Jewish neighbor to an inn for healing and recovery.

The surprising hero of Jesus' story is not a Jewish religious leader but a despised and often ostracized Samaritan. Though they all saw the ambushed man, only the Samaritan saw him as a neighbor in need. The religious bigotry and hypocrisy of the Levite and priest is contrasted with the true compassion of the Samaritan businessperson.

Indeed, as he tells this story, Jesus uses a very specific and important word to describe the Samaritan's motivation to help the injured man. This word expresses deep, heartfelt feelings of empathy often manifested physiologically. So deep are the feelings that those experiencing them are moved to loving action. It's worth noting that Jesus also uses this same word in the parable of the prodigal (Lk 15). There, Jesus intentionally highlights that the father, seeing his son return home after squandering his inheritance, is not angry or bitter but is moved by great empathy and generous love to help and care for his son. The word Jesus uses in Luke 10 and in Luke 15 is translated into modern English as *compassion*.[5]

A HEART OF COMPASSION

By using this specific word, the Gospel writer Luke is emphasizing that the loving Samaritan, unlike the two religious leaders, saw the robbed man neither as a Jew nor as a Samaritan, but rather as he would see his own needy son. The kind of compassion is a familial love. This is why the Samaritan cares for the man like a member of his own family. At the heart of his parable, Jesus insists that neighborly love is an extension of family love. A neighbor, properly understood, is a fellow image bearer of God, a member of the family of humanity.

In his surprising story Jesus showcases the amazing generosity of the Samaritan, who offers more than first aid but also leverages his resources to ensure the recovery of his injured neighbor. Like the generous father in the parable of the prodigal, who puts a ring on his son's finger, places shoes on his feet, and throws a lavish party to celebrate his return, the generous Samaritan businessman pulls out his credit card and guarantees payment for whatever the robbed and wounded man will need in this crisis.

In Jesus' story we observe a stark contrast between the callous indifference of the religious leaders and the heartfelt compassion of a Samaritan businessperson. However, we must not overlook another subtler contrast Jesus is making in the story. We need to pay attention to the contrast between the economic injustice of the robbers and the economic capacity and generosity of the Samaritan businessman. Embedded in Jesus' parable is an intentional contrast between the economic injustice perpetrated by the robbers, who wrongly take what is not theirs, and the economic goodness demonstrated by the Samaritan, who generously gives what is rightfully his.

Kenneth Bailey notes that Jesus' parable is literarily arranged into seven scenes, and argues that the first and final scenes present a clear economic contrast. Bailey writes, "In scene 1 the robbers take all the man's possessions, and in scene 7 the Samaritan pays for the man out of his own resources because the man has nothing."[6] Bailey's astute observation points us in the direction of an important truth built into Jesus' story: loving our neighbor in need involves both Christian compassion and economic capacity.

Jesus goes out of his way in this story to describe not only the merciful compassion of the Samaritan but also the economic generosity the Samaritan exhibited. Properly understood, neighborly love calls for truth, grace, and mercy to put on economic hands and feet.

Have we paused to consider how the Samaritan was able to care for his neighbor in this moment of crisis? What made it possible for the Samaritan businessperson to help his needy neighbor recover? The Samaritan was motivated by heartfelt compassion, but he was also able to engage in loving action because he had the economic capacity to do so. The Samaritan's economic capacity came from diligent labor and wise financial stewardship within an economic system where he added value to others. If we are going to love our neighbor well, we must not only manage our financial resources well; we must also have ample financial resources to manage. Distinguished economist Thomas Sowell emphasizes the need for economic capacity in caring for our neighbors. "Ultimately it is economic prosperity which makes possible for billions of dollars to be devoted to the less fortunate."[7] Compassion needs capacity if we are to care well for our neighbors.

The gospel both compels and empowers us with robust neighborly love. The apostle Paul makes the salient point as he describes how the gospel transforms not only our work but also our economic life, stating, "Let the thief no longer steal, but rather let him labor, doing honest work with his own hands, so that he may have something to share with anyone in need" (Eph 4:28).

Do we grasp what Paul is saying? The gospel not only addresses our greatest impoverishment, which is spiritual impoverishment resulting from our ruptured relationship with God, but also empowers us to address economic impoverishment in neighborly love.

The gospel compels us to live in such a God-honoring way that we do honest work, make an honest profit, and cultivate economic capacity to serve others and help meet their economic needs. Our diligent work creates economic value, and economic value leads to economic capacity for living generously.

THE BEST WORKERS MAKE THE BEST NEIGHBORS

The great sixteenth-century Protestant Reformer Martin Luther said it well, "God does not need your good works, but our neighbor does."[8] A primary way God designed us to love our neighbors is for us to do our work well, and from our work to have the capacity to be generous to neighbors in need. When it comes to being a helpful neighbor, a slothful worker faces an uphill climb. On the other hand, the best workers make the best neighbors.

As apprentices of Jesus we are called to be generous with our time and our talents. We are called to be generous with acts of kindness and faithful in our prayers for others. We are commissioned to be generous in sharing the gospel with our neighbors, and we are also called to be generous with our financial resources, which come from diligent labor and wise financial management. How can we be generous in tangibly caring for our neighbor if we have nothing to be generous with? If we have compassion without capacity, we have human frustration. If we have capacity without compassion, we have human alienation. If we have compassion and capacity, we have human transformation. We have neighborly love.

Dallas Willard adds thoughtful insight:

> The task of Christian spokespersons, leaders, and professionals is to exemplify and teach foundational traits of the good life Jesus manifests. But this must also include the more specific traits required in the public domain—industriousness,

self-control, moderation, and responsibility for oneself and others. That is the responsibility and posture of love. The human drive to be self-supporting can be tied to a determination to be productive in order to bless others.[9]

The Great Commandment challenges us to better connect Sunday to Monday, not only by nurturing compassionate hearts but also by growing in our economic capacity. And economic capacity does not appear out of thin air. It comes from our faithful vocational stewardship. The financial margin we need for generosity flows from a lifestyle of wise financial management. Neighborly love requires both compassion and capacity. It requires transformed hearts and habits, deep compassion, and faithful stewardship.

If we are going to narrow the Sunday-to-Monday gap between our faith, our work, and the economic flourishing of our neighbors, we must take tangible steps to love with both greater compassion and increased capacity. But what does this look like?

Know your neighbor. First, to love our neighbors we must seek to know our neighbors. Ask yourself, *Who are the neighbors in my life? Who are those I live by? Those I go to school with? Those I work with? What about those society says are not my neighbors? Those who speak a different language? Those who embrace different faiths? Those who live in another part of the city?* Geographic proximity calls for responsibility, but in a globalized world there is more than geographical proximity; there is also human proximity.

For many of us the ever-present danger of cultural insularity and isolation is quite real. We can be blinded to the economic difficulties experienced by our neighbors, even in communities minutes away from where we live. I was reminded of this truth when my wife, Liz, and I, who live in the suburbs of Kansas City, took an extended walk through one of the most underresourced neighborhoods in our metro area. Walking down Prospect Avenue, dilapidated storefronts and neglected vacant lots border the crumbling sidewalks. Viable businesses are virtually nonexistent. The lack of thriving stores or markets has made this area an urban food desert. Pride of ownership, meaningful work, and economic activity seem to have ground to a halt. The scene is heartbreaking and unfortunately not uncommon.

My wife and I have lived in Kansas City for over twenty-five years, yet before we intentionally walked through this neighborhood, we had no idea who these neighbors were, how they lived, or what challenges they faced in their neighborhoods. In many ways we had been hauntingly similar to the Jewish priest and Levite who walked past their neighbors in need. For years we not only walked past them, we avoided their neighborhood completely. This needs to change.

If we are going to embrace neighborly love, we will have to take the initiative to move out of the comfort zone of our cultural and geographical insularity and get to know our neighbors as people who, like us, have a unique history, have felt the pain of heartache, harbor unfulfilled dreams, and possess underutilized talents and future aspirations.

Help your neighbor. Once we've identified our neighbors, we can take tangible steps to help them. The first step will likely require us to increase our capacity to help. Think with me for a moment: How much good could the Samaritan have done if he hadn't worked hard on Monday? When we think about helping our neighbors, we ought to think first about our own work and the value it creates for others. We should consider how the economic capacity our work produces not only makes possible material provision for our families and ourselves, but also gives us opportunity to come alongside the poor and underresourced.

The Bible speaks a great deal about our responsibility to care for the poor and vulnerable, but how do we do that? Robert Lupton offers insight into the complexities of human impoverishment, reminding us that in spite of our best intentions sometimes our philanthropic efforts can yield unintended consequences: "While we are very generous in charitable giving, much of that money is either wasted or actually harms the people it is targeted to help."[10] Instead of adhering to philanthropic models that dehumanize our neighbors by perpetuating impoverishment, Lupton advocates the cultivation of institutions and relationships that develop economic capacity.

As we seek to help our neighbors, we must remember that both the creation of wealth and the stewardship of economic capacity through diligent work need biblical love and wisdom to guide them. You cannot help your neighbor well if you do not understand economics well, because human flourishing and economic flourishing go hand in hand.

Do your work well. This means that neighborly love is more about how we work than where we live, more about how we use our time and resources than who happens to live next door. While the Samaritan incarnated neighborly love, so did the innkeeper, whose year-round business provided an important service for the traveler. Unlike the robbers who perpetrated economic injustice against the Jewish man, the innkeeper worked hard to maintain a helpful enterprise that served others' needs. God created us as his image bearers with work in mind. An important aspect of being an image bearer of God is to work and to create value by serving others within our collaborative economic system.

Certainly we followers of Jesus are far from perfect, inhabit broken workplaces, and play out our vocational roles within imperfect economic systems. Nevertheless, we must remember that in spite of the less-than-ideal work we might do, and in spite of the less-than-optimum environments of labor we inhabit, we are called to be agents of redemption, doing good work as an act of worship, while seeking to further the common good. Human work is not a solitary enterprise; it is woven into the fabric of human community's flourishing design. Doing our work well matters to God and to our neighbor. The best workers make for the best neighbors.

I received an email from a member of my congregation whose company does a good deal of international business. His email speaks volumes about neighborly love. Tim is a modern-day Samaritan businessperson, doing good work and loving his neighbors in India. He describes his last fifteen years working with a talented international workforce:

> What I have come to realize is that my position of influence puts me in a unique position as a Christian. My workers in India are decent, hardworking, college educated, and have a desire to live a good life. I pay a fair wage and offer a path to economic freedom. Many on the team are the first generation to graduate from college. They are mostly Hindu and Muslim. During my many visits to India, they've told me that my values seem different from many perceptions they have of Americans. I've been able to share my faith and values with a group that is willing to listen. My neighbors in India now have a larger stake in a stable world since they are connected to the world economy. Their prosperity trickles down into their community. And hopefully they see a little of the love of Jesus reflected through me.[11]

Yes, the best workers make for the best neighbors!

A SACRIFICIAL LOVE

Finally, we must not miss that the Samaritan businessman not only loved his neighbor with abundant financial generosity, but also risked his life for his neighbor. With all the hatred, bigotry, and prejudice Jews had toward Samaritans, taking an injured Jewish man to a hotel was no simple task for the Samaritan. Indeed, the Samaritan faced the very real possibility of a hostile reception. Kenneth Bailey decontextualizes the complexity of the situation, placing its characters in the nineteenth-century American West. "Suppose a Native American found a cowboy with two arrows in his back, placed the cowboy on his horse and rode into Dodge City. What kind of reception do you think he would receive?"[12]

While the risky compassion and generous capacity of the Samaritan is stunning, we dare not overlook the fact that in telling this story, Jesus is ultimately pointing to himself. Jesus, the ultimate loving Samaritan, would not only risk his life but also lay it down freely on the cross for our sake. No matter our physical health or our economic condition, we are that person beaten and left for dead. We are helpless and utterly without hope, and we need Christ's compassion and sacrifice. Jesus, the ultimate good neighbor, who took on human flesh and lived among us, had both the compassion and capacity to rescue us (Jn 1:14). Both in his faithful work at the carpentry shop and through his atoning work on the cross, he demonstrated the highest expression of neighborly love.

The world still needs love sweet love, but it also needs jobs sweet jobs. The world needs our work of neighborly love, which is made possible by a fruitful and productive life.

2

MADE TO FLOURISH

*Work supplies the physical, psychological, artistic,
and religious needs of communities extending to the ends of
the earth. Furthermore, through work, we create abundance
out of which we help meet the needs of others.*

VICTOR CLAAR, *ECONOMICS IN CHRISTIAN PERSPECTIVE*

*And God blessed them. And God said to them, "Be fruitful and
multiply and fill the earth and subdue it, and have dominion over
the fish of the sea and over the birds of the heavens and over
every living thing that moves on the earth."*

GENESIS 1:28

The movie *The Intern* did not win any Academy Awards, which is hardly surprising. Punchy blockbuster comedies rarely receive Hollywood's highest honors. But its message is nevertheless award worthy. In *The Intern*, actor Robert De Nero plays a seventy-year-old widowed retiree who realizes there is a massive hole in his life. After playing too many rounds of golf and embarking on numerous trips to see the grandchildren, he looks in the mirror and sees a glaring lack of meaning and purpose staring back. But what is he to do?

After stumbling onto an advertisement for an entrepreneurial online fashion company offering nonpaid internships, DeNiro's character applies. And guess what? He lands the job. *The Intern* evokes some big laughs, but it also explores a serious theme, engaging our human need to find meaning by both connecting with others and contributing to the world.

Not only recent movies engage this subject. In his classic twentieth-century work *Man's Search for Meaning*, psychiatrist and Holocaust survivor Viktor Frankl made the compelling case that humans are fundamentally meaning-seeking creatures. Frankl advocates we search for meaning in two quests of the human heart—intimacy and accomplishment. It is in the relationships we make and the work we do that meaning greets us. No matter our age, education, ethnicity, or gender, we long to contribute, to accomplish things, to make a difference, to live a flourishing life. But what does a flourishing life look like?

JESUS AND THE FLOURISHING LIFE

Jesus spoke a great deal about the truly good and flourishing life. In his most famous sermon, the Sermon on the Mount, Jesus charts the paradoxical terrain of the flourishing life, identifying what it is, where it is found, and how it is experienced for those who apprentice themselves to him. The Gospel writer John frames the flourishing life against the backdrop of Jesus the good Shepherd, whose continual presence, constant protection, and capable provision make possible the flourishing life. Recording the words of Jesus, John writes, "The thief comes only to steal and kill and destroy. I came that they may have life and have it abundantly" (Jn 10:10). Jesus, the sinless Son of God, came to our sin-ravaged planet so that we might flourish in all dimensions of our human existence. Tragically, we often reduce the richness of what Jesus came to accomplish, confining his pronouncements of flourishing to our own personalized, privatized, and pietistic faith.

Jesus' teaching on the Great Commandment reminds us that human flourishing is multidimensional, encompassing both our vertical relationship with God and our horizontal relationships with our neighbors. Flourishing lives matter a great deal to God and to our neighbors. The measure of our neighborly love is not only seen in our ever-increasing Christlike character, but also in our outpouring of Christlike compassion and productive capacity for the good of our neighbors. When we wholeheartedly embrace the Great Commandment, we are compelled to live with greater compassion and fruitful productivity, which fuel our economic capacity. As our economic capacity grows, whether it is measured in influence, access, or ownership of wealth, our ability to lead a life of love-fueled fruitfulness increases.

When we look back at God's original design for human flourishing, we discover we were created for a vibrant life of responsible creativity, innovation, and productivity. In and through these capacities, we were designed to reflect our Creator and to experience a deep sense of meaning as we express our love for God and for our neighbors in our productive work.

CREATED TO BE CREATIVE

If we are going to more fully grasp God's design and desire for human flourishing, we must learn the biblical story well, observing its seamless continuity and coherence. We must begin at the beginning. Few of us would see a movie or read a book and miss the beginning, yet so many of us do not take the time to look closely at the beginning of the biblical story. Whether we have studied the Bible extensively or read it only a little, the ever-present danger for each one of us is to see what we know rather than truly know what we see. With fresh eyes of curiosity and with sharp senses for close observation, let's go back to the beginning and explore God's creation design in the opening pages of the Bible.

In Genesis 1 we are immediately introduced to a God who works and is productive. As his masterful creational architecture unfolds, humankind emerges on the landscape of time as the sparkling crown of his magnificent achievement.

Then God said, "Let us make man in our image, after our likeness. And let them have dominion over the fish of the sea and over the birds of the heavens and over the livestock and over all the earth and over every creeping thing that creeps on the earth."

So God created man in his own image,
    in the image of God he created him;
        male and female he created them. (Gen 1:26-27)

On the sixth day of creation the biblical writer ushers us to a front-row seat to observe humanity's creation. Here we see something distinct in the biblical narrative. This distinction is emphasized in the threefold repetition of the word *image*. When we hear the word *image*, we may have an initial negative reaction. In our contemporary context, image language is often used in conjunction with individuals who display a kind of flaky lack of authenticity. We might imagine a politician who tries to look a certain way to earn votes, or a colleague at work or a peer at school who tries too hard to ramp up their cool factor. But what does this word mean in Genesis 1? Here, *image* doesn't convey a lack of authenticity. Rather, it connotes the opposite. The image language of Genesis 1 affirms the enduring stamp of our Creator on us—his authentic, created beings.

Being created in God's image means humans are endowed with two essential and unique characteristics in the created order. First, we were designed to experience relational connection with our relational God. Second, we were given the creative capacity to reflect God in all that we are and do. To borrow words from Frankl, the Genesis account reveals that we were made for intimacy and for accomplishment. Theologian John Kilner captures well what the word *image* conveys. "God creates humanity in reference to (according to) the likeness-image of God. That concept involves humanity's special connection with God, which makes possible for humanity to become a meaningful reflection of God."[1]

Because humans are created in God's image, we have unimaginable intrinsic worth. Being made in God's image means that our lives matter both in who we are and what we do. We were designed to connect with God relationally and to reflect God in our work. In this sense we are both human beings and human doings. Our relational connection with God is essential for us to reflect him. Without connection, there is little reflection. Human flourishing is first and foremost a flourishing of relationships—our relationship with God and with others. But human flourishing is also a product of fruitful work that reflects our God who works.

REFLECTING THE GOD WHO WORKS

In Genesis 1 we see that the God we were made to reflect is a productive, fruitful, and creative worker. Parents and grandparents particularly delight when they see creativity budding in their children and grandchildren. Watching children explore the world, we marvel at the many ways children's fertile imaginations are ignited. We capture the creativity of their play on our cell phones. The pictures they draw quickly end up on our refrigerator doors. The castles and jet fighters they make, the cardboard forts they erect in the basement or in the backyard, enrich our lives in inexpressible ways.

I love watching young boys and girls build things with Legos. Their small, creative masterpieces cannot help but reflect their image-bearing nature and remind us we were all made to make things. When I think of creation's design, it is as if God made the world and gave us a massive pile of Legos to play with for our sense of accomplishment, the well-being of our neighbors, and for his glory. We did not create the Legos themselves, but we have been entrusted to steward well the Legos we've been given, and we need to recognize that those pieces are brimming with seemingly endless possibilities.

When we make things, we reflect God and express love for our neighbor. No matter our age, God created us to be creative, to serve others, and to work. Yet many of us are all too quick to dismiss or minimize our creativity. If we are not an accomplished musician, a notable artist, a Hollywood star, a Steve Jobs in business, or a Nobel Prize winner in economics or literature, we may discount our creativity. To minimize our unique creativity is to diminish the God who designed us in his image. Each one of us has the capacity to be creative and to reflect God with our creative output.

Some people are amazing at starting new business enterprises or managing existing complex commercial ventures. Others can make beautiful meals. Some folks can design or build almost anything. As someone who is technologically challenged, I stand in awe of those who are breathtakingly creative in solving computer problems. Creativity is a capacity we all have, and we are wise to take seriously its stewardship. God made us to be creative not only to reflect him but also to use that creativity for loving our neighbor. We were created to be creative, and we are also called to fruitfulness.

OUR CULTURAL MANDATE

On the sixth day of creation we read, "And God blessed them. And God said to them, 'Be *fruitful* and *multiply* and *fill* the earth and *subdue* it, and *have dominion* over the fish of the sea and over the birds of the heavens and over every living thing that moves on the earth'"

(Gen 1:28, italics added). Theologians often call this biblical text the cultural mandate, which is like our human job description, our earthly responsibility as image bearers of God. It is what we were created to do, what we are entrusted to get done in the world. The cultural mandate might also be understood as God's "get to work" mandate.

Unlike the rest of creation, humans are given great capacity to creatively make things, as well as the responsibility to create and steward cultures themselves. Artist Makoto Fujimura speaks about the implications of the cultural mandate, as well as our stewardship responsibility to care for culture. "Culture care is everyone's business," and "It's not enough to have artists who seek after beauty, truth, and goodness; we must have churches, policies, and communities that promote a long-term nurture of culture that is beautiful, truthful, and full of goodness."[2] Fujimura rightly reminds us to take seriously our cultural mandate. Faithful, fruitful, and flourishing lives nurture vibrant flourishing cultures.

Within the unfolding biblical story the cultural mandate is of greater importance and more far-reaching in its scope than we may at first realize. In Genesis 1 we find five imperative words strung together like interlocking links on a chain (*be fruitful, multiply, fill, subdue,* and *have dominion*). Linguistically, imperatives are authoritative commands, not optional suggestions. Like the locomotive on a train, the first imperative in the cultural mandate, "be fruitful," pulls the lion's share of the weight, while the other imperatives follow, adding greater breadth of understanding to what the author is trying to communicate. What does the writer have in mind when he writes of humans' responsibility to be fruitful?

When we hear the command "Be fruitful!" we tend to think of having babies, maybe even lots of babies. And of course an important part of the human job description is producing offspring. But we must not miss that the cultural mandate addresses much more than merely having babies. The Hebrew word translated in

English as "be fruitful" certainly connotes procreativity but also carries with it the idea of productivity.[3] The five imperatives in the cultural mandate bear witness to this important truth. The immediate context of Genesis 1 affirms this, and Genesis 2 reinforces that the writer comprehensively understands fruitfulness as more than just bearing children.

One way to rightly understand the fruitfulness humans were designed for is to look at the way their fruitfulness is thwarted after the first humans' sin. When sin enters the world in Genesis 3, God's perfect creation design is massively corrupted. As a result, we see human fruitfulness in all its dimensions severely affected. Both Adam and Eve's procreativity and productivity become painful and toilsome (Gen 3:16-19). As a result of sin, humankind's ability to carry out the cultural mandate is made difficult.

Fruitfulness is defined by both procreativity and productivity beyond Genesis 3. In the book of Deuteronomy the Hebrew word for fruitfulness is used to describe the procreativity and productivity of God's covenant people. Language of cursing and blessing frames the consequences of obedience and disobedience to God. The writer of Deuteronomy describes the comprehensive flourishing and fruitful living God desires for his covenant people. "Blessed shall be the fruit of your womb and the fruit of your ground and the fruit of your cattle, the increase of your herds and the young of your flock" (Deut 28:4). We must not miss that fruitfulness is described not only in terms of fruitfulness of procreativity, the fruit of the womb, but also the fruitfulness of *productivity*, the fruit of the ground, the fruit of your cattle.

The book of Proverbs also uses the Hebrew word for fruitfulness to speak about economic productivity and the financial generosity that comes from our work, describing generous giving as our "firstfruits" (Prov 3:9).

If we take the time to understand the cultural mandate, we see being fruitful means more than simply having children; it also speaks to productive human work. One of the distorted messages often presented to people who are single, or to those who do not have children, is that their lives are incomplete. But let's remember Jesus, who was the sinless incarnation and perfect embodiment of divinity and humanity, never had children. While not all of us can be procreative, each of us can be productive. Every one of us can add value to others, cultivating blessing from the created order while being faithful to God's specific calling for our lives. Even the most physically handicapped bearer of God's image can lead a fruitful life of contribution to the created order.

Another tragic consequence of an impoverished understanding of the cultural mandate is that women's value and contribution to human flourishing is often minimized. Many women who face infertility or who have been called to a single life have languished under a reductionist understanding that a woman's fruitfulness derives from having and caring for children. Katelyn Beaty rightly reminds us, "Every human being is made to work. And since women are human beings, every woman is made to work."[4] A central thread woven in the brilliant tapestry of the creation narrative is the divine design and mandate for human productivity.

HUMAN FLOURISHING AND ECONOMIC VALUE

The Genesis creation account makes it abundantly clear we were created with work in mind. Whether our work is paid or not paid, our work is to glorify God, honor others, and add value to their lives.[5] One of the primary ways we live into God's creation design is by living a flourishing life of God-honoring productivity. From cradle to grave we were created to live a fruitful life. Looking through the lens of Holy Scripture, human work must be seen first and foremost as value contribution, not economic compensation.

We can have a flourishing, fruitful life even if we don't get a paycheck, because fruitfulness is about cultivating blessing from the created order. Fruitfulness means adding value and bestowing honor to others in and through our work. Fruitfulness is building up and utilizing our capacity for influence, access, and wealth so we might tangibly express our neighborly love. We may retire from our paycheck, but we never retire from work. We never retire from the privilege and responsibility of neighborly love.

While human flourishing is more than creativity and productivity, it is not less than this. Productivity is a vital aspect of fruitfulness, and our productivity often brings with it economic value through which we love our neighbor within a monetized economic system. When we hear the word *economics*, we may think of spreadsheets or supply and demand graphs. We may think of various economic theories or schools of thought. We might think of financial news outlets or national trade policies. But at its heart, economics is merely the study of the economy, and the economy, as Greg Forster so eloquently writes, is simply "the social system through which people organize their work and dispose of its fruits."[6]

Though economists tend to deal with lots of theory and empirical data, some economists, like Victor Claar and Robin Klay, insightfully translate the complex world of economics, helping us understand our everyday life in the context of our global economy. Claar and Klay aptly note:

> Through work we take care of our families and ourselves; we collaborate with others by working together to create good things. Today, more than ever before our work depends on a vast web of collaboration. Work supplies the physical, psychological, artistic and religious needs of communities extending to the ends of the earth. Furthermore, through work, we create abundance out of which we help meet the needs of others.[7]

Economists remind us the work we do matters much more than we often realize. Scripture also informs us that our productivity or lack thereof matters to God, to us, and to our neighbors.

Recognizing the importance of fruitful productivity, Living Hope Church in Chicago is committed to creating opportunities for community members to increase their vocational fruitfulness. Located in Chicago's South Side, Living Hope is pastored by Brad Beier. The church serves a community with an unemployment rate of 23 percent. Recognizing an opportunity to care well for their neighbors, Living Hope has sought ways to provide meaningful work to those surrounding the church. Pastor Beier has also articulated a philosophy of benevolence that insists neighbors who want money or help should be given work to do by the church. In addition, Living Hope has started a nonprofit economic development ministry called Hope Works.

Hope Works focuses specifically on economic empowerment and job creation. The organization provides on-ramps for participants to engage in church ministry, relationship building, and discipleship. Lives are being transformed, families are being put back together, and the dignity of doing good work is once again being validated in a community where joblessness and crime has been the norm. Living Hope is increasingly seen in the community as a place where people find spiritual hope as well as economic vitality.

Living Hope is doing important work that affirms the goodness of productivity and empowers others to lead fruitful lives. As God's image bearers we were created to be fruitful. We are not to worship our work, but our work is a vital aspect of our worship. Our hands and bodies were designed to work and to pray in a seamless life of God-focused and God-directed worship. We were made to add value to the world in and through our work, and to love our neighbor in and through our fruitfulness.

3

HUMAN FRUITFULNESS AND MATERIAL WEALTH

If silver and gold are things evil in themselves,

then those who keep away from them deserve to be

praised. But if they are good creations of God, which we

can use both for the needs of our neighbor and for the glory

of God, is not a person silly, yes, even unthankful to God,

if he refrains from them as though they were evil?

MARTIN LUTHER, *LECTURES ON GENESIS*

No one can serve two masters, for either he will hate the one and

love the other, or he will be devoted to the one and despise

the other. You cannot serve both God and money.

MATTHEW 6:24

I f we are to love our neighbors in accordance with Jesus' teaching, heartfelt compassion and economic capacity are both needed. Our neighborly love requires economic hands and feet. We understand this practically, and see it affirmed biblically. Yet so often, as I engage in pastoral conversations with those in the church I serve, I am greeted with a sincere question: Isn't economic capacity bad? "Pastor Tom, I certainly understand that loving our neighbors well requires resources, but didn't Jesus caution us about wealth?"

Their question is hardly surprising. Indeed, many of us might hold negative opinions toward wealth. We may think of wealth as something someone else has (and perhaps something we want too). We might be quick to assume that wealth is unspiritual or only comes through exploitative enterprise. But properly understood, wealth simply refers to something of value. Indeed, while theologians use words like *flourishing* and *fruitfulness* to speak of adding value to the world, economists use words like *productivity*, *opportunity*, and *wealth*. Wealth creation in all its dimensions is a vital part of our creation design and cultural mandate. Indeed, wealth creation is something we are created and called to do in the world.

Cultural observer Andy Crouch makes the salient point that God invites us into the creative process and actually allows us to add value to the world, to create wealth by making better things than God made in the original creation. Andy Crouch says, "God made wheat. We make bread! God made grapes. We make wine. Wheat is good. Bread is very good! Grapes are good, but wine—that is very good."[1] Think about it: we take sand and make computer chips. We take trees and make furniture and paper. Whether the value we create with our time and energy is monetized or not, we create wealth in the world. A wealthy and generous God designed us with that in mind. Yet in many Christian circles the idea of material wealth or wealth creation quickly gets a black eye.

TWO VIEWS OF WEALTH

Throughout the history of the church there have been two prominent and diverging views of wealth. One view insists that wealth and material wealth creation are intrinsically corrupting and therefore must be avoided at all cost. This view contends that the right path for the true Christian is to renounce all wealth. The other view contends that material wealth and wealth creation are essentially good and are part of our creation design and cultural mandate. In its best forms this view admits that wealth can be perilous in our fallen world, while nevertheless advocating that wealth must not be avoided but rather carefully stewarded in love for God and our neighbor.

Pointing to the early church sources for these contrasting views, historian Peter Brown writes,

> Wealth had been problematized. But it had not been demonized. Few Christian thinkers of the later fifth and sixth centuries thought that wealth should be rejected out of hand. . . . To this was added the dry view upheld by later Augustinians that wealth itself was a gift of God that demanded forms of management as strict and as careful as that exercised by any procurator on an imperial estate.[2]

Today, in many Christian circles, wealth is seen as anything but a gift to steward well. I find this unfortunate, because I am persuaded that the Augustinian view is the conclusion best supported by Scripture. Indeed, I believe material wealth is a gift rather than a curse.

The poverty gospel. However we understand wealth or value creation, and the monetary exchange and allocation that often accompany it, there are two common and dangerous distortions advocated under the banner of Christian teaching. The first distortion is what we might call the poverty gospel. Underlying many manifestations of the poverty gospel is a contemporary form of gnosticism, which devalues the true goodness of the material world. The poverty gospel often fuels a blinding, pietistic spiritual pride that asserts the greater the material poverty, the more spiritual the person. Inherent in this distorted biblical teaching is that material poverty brings spiritual riches, and material abundance inevitably brings spiritual poverty.

Proponents of the poverty gospel are right to remind us of many biblical texts that speak to the sizeable dangers that accompany increasing material wealth. They also rightly call an increasingly affluent Western church to greater material generosity and deeper sacrificial living (see Mt 6:24; 19:16-30; 1 Tim 6:7-10; Heb 13:5). Yet those who embrace the poverty gospel in its many explicit and implicit forms make a theological error by too closely wedding evil with material prosperity. Dallas Willard exposes the dangerous poverty gospel. "The idealization of poverty is one of the most dangerous illusions of Christians in the contemporary world. Stewardship which requires possessions and includes giving is the true spiritual discipline in relation to wealth."[3] Material impoverishment is no more intrinsically spiritual than material abundance. In all economic circumstances, whether they are bleak or bright, faithful and fruitful stewardship of all God entrusts is required.

The prosperity gospel. A second dangerous distortion regarding material wealth is the prosperity gospel. Proponents of the prosperity gospel believe the creation of wealth is an authenticating sign or a direct causal apologetic for God's blessing. Prosperity gospel adherents assert that God wants everyone to be materially prosperous.[4] Embedded in the prosperity gospel is a good and admirable attention to what is often a neglected robust theology of the goodness of human flourishing.

Tragically, like most theological distortions, important truth is ignored, minimized, or outright denied. In many cases, prosperity gospel proponents have a paltry view of human suffering, tend to ignore Scripture's call to a sacrificial lifestyle fueled by neighborly love, and blatantly disregard the sovereign will of God for some of Jesus' followers to experience material poverty. While affirming some of the good aspects of prosperity-gospel teaching, John Schneider persuasively challenges its basic premise that God desires all to be materially prosperous: "It is that there are not times or circumstances in this world in which God, would on balance, prefer someone to be poor. And Scripture makes very clear that such times and circumstances often do exist."[5] The prosperity gospel is not only inconsistent with Scripture, it also flies in the face of many devoted followers of Jesus in the present day and throughout church history who face and have faced great material deprivation in their apprenticeship with Jesus.

On Christmas Eve in Tehran, house-church pastor Farshid Fatah and his family were awakened to the frightening sounds of the Iranian security police pounding at their door. After the police searched his apartment and seized his computer, Farshid was arrested and sent to Evin prison. Farshid's crime was being a follower of Jesus. Behind bars and often in solitary confinement, Farshid was deprived of his freedom, his material possessions, and his livelihood. For six years, Farshid had very limited contact with his family, yet in the midst of the crucible of material and relational deprivation, Farshid lived a God-honoring flourishing life. In a note sent from prison, Farshid described his difficult experience as a lovely wilderness where his good Shepherd was with him. Like many other members of the persecuted church around the globe, Farshid's story reminds us that even in the most difficult circumstances and times of relational and material deprivation, followers of Jesus can and do flourish.

A closer examination of Jesus' teaching as well as other biblical texts reveals a parting of company with both the poverty gospel and the prosperity gospel. Jesus calls us to a life of humble dependence on him to be our provider and protector. No matter our circumstances we are called to the wise stewardship of material wealth in an obedient lifestyle of diligent work, fruitfulness, productivity, and responsibility.

A FIXED PIE OR A GROWING PIE?

Seeing that wealth is neither to be avoided nor praised but rather stewarded wisely and generously, how should we think about material wealth creation? This is an important question worthy of thoughtful biblical and economic reflection. And it is preceded by another: Is material wealth a static or dynamic realty? Sometimes we assume there is a "fixed pie" of wealth or fruitfulness in the world. When we embrace this idea, we tend to believe that because there is only one wealth pie, and because that pie can only be divided into so many pieces, we must cut smaller and smaller slices so everyone can have a bite of roughly the same size.

From a perceptual perspective, daily economic life in biblical times was pretty much a zero-sum game.[6] Though the potential for remarkable growth in wealth existed—as it always does when creative image bearers are free to innovate in God's abundant creation—technological limits, agrarian focus, and the lack of legal protections and basic human rights prevented great advances. Grasping this helps us read the biblical text through a more culturally clarifying lens.

A robust theology of creation, however, helps us see the error of the fixed-pie view. God designed the natural created order so the wealth pie might be expanded through human work.[7] The common fixed-pie fallacy suggests that one person's growth in wealth results in another person's diminishing wealth. This is untrue both on micro- and macroeconomic levels. Economist Thomas Sowell speaks with illuminating clarity, "Many economic fallacies are due to conceiving of economic activity as a zero-sum contest, in which what is gained by one is lost by another. This in turn is often due to ignoring the fact that wealth is created in the course of economic activity."[8]

Despite a robust theology of creation design, growing awareness that human wealth creation benefits the common good, and increasing awareness of economic principles, somehow the fixed-pie notion stubbornly persists in our broader culture and in the church. The effects of this fallacy in the contemporary pulpit are evident. Both explicitly and implicitly many preaching pastors herald the notion that the wealthy create the poor in a causal kind of relationship. Speaking of this historical Pelagian influence, Peter Brown writes, "In his [Pelagius's] view, the distribution of wealth and poverty in society was the result of an unforgiving zero-sum game. Those who went beyond the measure of sufficiency could do so only by taking from the poor. Excess in the few automatically led to dispossession of the many."[9]

Is there a fixed pie of wealth and fruitfulness in the world? The key principle we see both in the cultural mandate and in economic theory is that wealth creation is an exponential dynamic. This means the work of cultivating the Garden of Eden was a call to steward the raw materials of God's creation and to create something that wasn't there before, multiplying it many times over for the flourishing of all (Gen 2:15).

I am reminded of the exponential dynamic of fruitful productivity when I see signs along the roadside in the breadbasket states of our country. Signs like "One Kansas or Nebraska farmer feeds 70 people and you!" Whether it is food production, energy extraction, or digital platform technology, it is stunning to think of the creation of value and wealth that has occurred in our world. It is also amazing to think of the way innovation has created even more wealth. Today, with digital platform technology, the world's largest taxi company, Uber, owns no vehicles. The world's largest media owner, Facebook, creates no intellectual content. The most valuable retailer, Alibaba, has no inventory. The world's largest accommodation provider, Airbnb, owns no real estate.[10] This is remarkable indeed.

As a teenager I remember reading the acclaimed book *The Population Bomb*, a bestseller out of Stanford University. The thesis of the book was that the world's growing population would experience mass starvation in the 1980s as food production was predicted to hit its ceiling. Yet when we look back on a world population that has grown from 1.8 billion at the turn of the twentieth century to 7.3 billion today, we see how *The Population Bomb* was a huge bust. Why was this fearful fixed-pie scarcity idea so wrong? A look back at economic history is helpful in gaining needed perspective.

A LOOK BACK AT ECONOMIC HISTORY

When economic historians examine history they often depict the economic activity and material well-being of humanity as looking like a hockey stick.[11] If we were to portray the historical development of human economic activity on an x-y axis graph it would look like a hockey stick. For the vast majority of human history, people lived relatively short lifespans in vulnerable and often subsistence economic contexts. But then, around 1800, the extended flat line began to change and take a dramatic turn upward. Economic historian Deirdre McCloskey writes,

> Economic history has looked like an ice-hockey stick lying on the ground. It had a long, long horizontal handle at $3 a day extending through the two-hundred-thousand-year history of Homo sapiens to 1800, with little bumps upward on the handle in ancient Rome and the early medieval Arab world and high medieval Europe, with regressions to $3 afterward— then a wholly unexpected blade, leaping up in the last two

out of the two thousand centuries to $30 a day and in many places well beyond.[12]

McCloskey coined the term "the Great Enrichment" to refer to the rapid economic transformation throughout the West and much of the world since the 1800s.[13] Swedish public health professor Hans Rosling has persuasively illustrated the hockey stick of global economic betterment by tracking increasing human physical health and life expectancy.[14] On the heels of the Industrial Revolution, many nations who had been poor and sick for millennia began to flourish as a result of economic betterment. Though there continue to be pockets of poor and sick nations, and though wealth disparity continues to be a big challenge, Hans Rosling traces the trend line of modern history, enthusiastically pointing to progress being made today.

So what happened in history that so dramatically changed humanity's material well-being? How are we to understand this period of great economic enrichment, which typifies our late modern world? Some have suggested that the advances and flourishing experienced during "the Great Enrichment" were enabled by economic injustice. These critics point to dignity-defacing practices like slavery and colonization, suggesting these evils were the actual drivers of wealth creation. However, since the 1950s, when decolonization began in earnest and communism began to lose its hold in many national governments, the rate of enrichment has only increased. This suggests that economically exploitative, morally evil practices were not the key drivers of economic advancement.

Deirdre McCloskey explains the remarkable rise in the global standard of living by looking to factors outside of economics, such as the emerging ideas of "liberty and dignity for ordinary people."[15] Michael Novak looks to a triad of transformational ideas including moral, political, and economic factors he labels as civic republicanism and democratic capitalism. Novak writes,

> A new political ideal was born: that of the commercial republic. Such a republic called for new virtues of civic republicanism: the seizing of personal responsibility and new habits of self-government in both private and in public life. . . . For human liberty and human flourishing are fulfilled by neither politics alone nor economics alone. Rather they require economic activity within a free polity, under the rule of law, and through the daily practice of personal habits of wisdom and self control.[16]

Hernando de Soto makes the case that the formation of legal property rights laws provided an engine of capital development and human economic incentive. De Soto writes,

> Law began adapting to the needs of common people, including their expectations about property rights, in most Western European countries during the nineteenth and early twentieth centuries. . . . Politicians finally understood that the problem was not people, but the law which was discouraging and preventing people from being more productive.[17]

My sense is that likely a combination of spiritual, moral, cultural, political, legal, and technological factors has influenced the rapid trajectory of human economic betterment in the last two hundred years. It is very encouraging that in the last decade, an innovative, market-oriented, globalized economy has lifted about one billion people in the world from desperate poverty.[18] Of course there is much more to do. Abuses and inequities within the system must be addressed. Theoretical and practical differences remain concerning the wisest path forward, particularly as we wrestle with how best to understand the increase in wealth disparity we are observing. But nevertheless, "the Great Enrichment" should excite us.

Even so, I believe we must also pause and reflect on the unintended negative consequences of a more materially abundant and comfortable life. While having better physical health and increased economic well-being is a welcome facet of human flourishing, humanity's grave spiritual impoverishment and alienation from God calls for bold gospel proclamation and incarnation. With greater material abundance also comes greater responsibility for wise stewardship, abundant generosity, and planetary sustainability. Jesus' sobering reminder "to whom much was given, . . . much will be required" (Lk 12:48) is both a timely and timeless word in this time of human economic betterment.

Both material poverty and material wealth bring challenges. Greed is a temptation for all economic contexts, for greed does not depend on how much we may have, but on how much of what we may have has us. Pride, greed, and corruption can attach themselves to both the materially rich and the materially poor. The book of Proverbs speaks a great deal about the dangers of both poverty and wealth. When it comes to material wealth, the writer of Proverbs recites the prayer of the wise.

Give me neither poverty nor riches;
feed me with the food that is needful for me,
lest I be full and deny you
and say "Who is the Lord?"
or lest I be poor and steal
and profane he name of my God. (Prov 30:8-9)

Proverbs also speaks a great deal about the danger of slothfulness and a lack of productivity. We must be careful to avoid two dead-end roads of faulty thinking. On the one hand, we may be tempted to think that those who don't have as much as we do are lazy or don't have enough faith. On the other hand, we may convince ourselves that those who have more than we do are greedy and selfish. As a gospel-centered people, we need to see our own spiritual impoverishment and human bankruptcy, and to remember that our sinful hearts need the gospel whether we find ourselves with much or with little.

ARE WE FLOURISHING?

In Genesis we are reminded that we were created with community in mind. We were created to flourish, to be fruitful, to add value to others in the world. We also see wealth creation as a good thing, because through it, we reflect our created nature and have an increased capacity to love our neighbor. Writing to the Philippians, the apostle Paul reflects on his fruitful life. Paul greatly anticipated his eternal destiny yet focuses on his life calling with the anticipation of more fruitful labor in the days ahead: "If I am to live in the flesh, that means fruitful labor for me" (Phil 1:22).

A flourishing life of fruitfulness matters. Frederick Buechner reminds us of the importance of our calling to fruitfulness and makes the point there is "a place where the world's hunger and your gladness meet."[19] Each one of us is designed to make a difference, to contribute to God's good world, and to our neighbor's well-being. Being productive in our work within our economic system—flawed and imperfect as it may be—is an important way we bear God's image and love others.

Whatever work God has called us to, we must ask: Are we becoming more fruitful workers? Are we increasingly doing our job better and gaining greater skill? If we are in a paid work context, what kind of job reviews are we getting? If we are pursuing more formal education, are we taking our learning seriously? We may be in a season or station in life where we are not getting a regular paycheck. How are we continuing to grow in our contribution to others? Growing our fruitfulness may mean more time for prayer or for volunteering in the community or our local church. It might mean writing notes to others or other tangible acts of kindness, or caring for our grandchildren.

If we are a stay-at-home spouse, are we becoming a more fruitful parent? Do we realize our most important neighbors are the children we are raising? Every scriptural imperative that speaks of loving our neighbor as we love ourselves certainly comes to bear on how we parent. Every command to love preferentially at great cost, with great effort, and with godly wisdom is not merely a command to love the people in our workplace, in our church, on our street, or in the homeless shelter. Rather, every command becomes a command to love the people under our own roof, no matter how small. If children are people, then our own children are our closest neighbors. No other neighbor lives closer or needs our self-sacrificing love more.

The gospel speaks to the productive work we do every day within the economic system we inhabit. Our seamless gospel faith tells us that every nook and cranny of our lives matters. Our economic choices are overflowing with spiritual significance. The fruitful lives we are called to have profound economic implications for our world. As apprentices of Jesus, the mandate to bear much fruit in every dimension of our lives is at the heart of faithful Christian discipleship.

4

THE FRUITFULNESS OF FAITHFULNESS

Leadership positions in our society must provide the means for both moral fulfillment and productive flourishing. Not just one, but both these objectives must be uniformly valued and pursued.

DALLAS WILLARD, *THE DIVINE CONSPIRACY CONTINUED*

By this my Father is glorified, that you bear much fruit and so prove to be my disciples.

JOHN 15:8

Napa, California, is one of my favorite places to visit. I love feeling the temperate warmth of its Mediterranean-style climate, taking in its lush valleys and deep blue skies, and enjoying the laid back lifestyle. Napa is not only a beautiful place to visit; it is also a great place to grow things—especially grapes. Some of the finest wines in the world come from the Napa Valley region.

Every wine tasting I've experienced there only solidifies that conclusion.

The farmers who grow the many varieties of grapes in Napa Valley inevitably talk in detail about the importance of each microclimate's unique soil composition. Different soils produce different grapes, and different grapes make different wines. Though I have never grown grapes, I know if you are going to get really good wine, it is imperative to have really good soil. Good soil produces good fruit.

The Napa Valley farmers' knowledge about making wine and Jesus' knowledge about human flourishing have striking similarities. Jesus asserted that what is true of the soil beneath us is true of the soul within us. When it comes to living a fruitful life, the condition of the human soul matters. Like good soils, good souls yield fruitful lives.

Throughout his teaching ministry Jesus emphasized the undeniable reality that those who embrace him, who faithfully obey his teaching and apprentice their lives to him, will bear much fruit. He spoke often of the goodness of fruitfulness and said his followers' fruit would distinguish them as true disciples.

So often, we are encouraged in our personal journeys of discipleship to lead more faithful lives marked by obedience and trust. And certainly faithfulness is an essential component of true discipleship. Without faith, we cannot know God or please God. Our enduring, trusting, persevering faithfulness matters. Yet, in our pursuit of faithfulness, I wonder if we might not have unintentionally overlooked the high importance of fruitfulness, missing the comprehensive fullness of what God desires for us. In fact, I'd go so far as to ask: Is it possible to lead a faithful life without leading a fruitful life? Can we be faithful without being fruitful?

For Jesus, evidence of authentic followership manifested itself in authenticating fruitfulness. And our fruitfulness is of such importance to Jesus that he shed his innocent blood so that we might lead fruitful lives. Indeed, the good news of the gospel is that Jesus came not only to save our souls but to redeem his broken creation and to transform all aspects of human existence. The gospel shines the light of grace and truth into every nook and cranny of life. It is the good and powerful news of the gospel that makes human flourishing possible. The gospel empowers us to rightly love God and our neighbor, and makes us into new persons who foster virtuous and vibrant social ecosystems, with moral and innovative economies (2 Cor 5:17). Jesus came not only to save us from our lives of sin but also to save us for lives of flourishing and fruitfulness.

On the night before his crucifixion, Jesus gathered his disciples around him. In their final moments together, Jesus not only washed his disciples' feet but also gave them words of encouragement and instruction. Jesus' words, recorded in the Gospel of John, are often referred to as the Upper Room Discourse by theologians. During this intimate conversation, Jesus calls his disciples to live fruitful lives.

ABIDING AND FRUITFULNESS

The Gospel writer John welcomes his readers to get up close and personal as Jesus transparently shares his heart with his disciples. Like he has already done with his teaching on the yoke and the cross, Jesus once again follows the rabbinical pattern of invitation, metaphor, and paradox.[1] Like the cross and the yoke, the allegorical metaphor of the vine and its branches points the way to the truly good life of human fruitfulness and flourishing.

Even a cursory observation of the first half of John 15 reveals a close connection between the two constantly repeated words *abide* and *fruit*. As Jesus extends an invitation to the fruitful life, he makes clear that such a life is found in him, the Creator and

Redeemer of all things. Jesus says, "Abide in me, and I in you. As the branch cannot bear fruit by itself, unless it abides in the vine, neither can you, unless you abide in me" (Jn 15:4). Lest we miss the full thrust of Jesus' teaching, it is important to see the explicit and exclusive truth claim he makes to his disciples. "I am the vine; you are the branches. Whoever abides in me and I in him, he it is that bears much fruit, for apart from me you can do nothing" (Jn 15:5). The very night before Jesus goes to the cross as the sinless Lamb of God, he speaks about the vital importance of human fruitfulness and identifies himself as its exclusive source. But what precisely does Jesus have in mind?

Jesus' teaching on the importance and source of human fruitfulness must not be analyzed in isolation but rather engaged as it emerges within the coherent arch of the larger biblical story. Jesus is connecting the original cultural mandate to bear fruit with the restored fruit bearing of redemption, which will be made possible by his atoning work on the cross and his glorious resurrection. Moses and the people of Israel wandered for forty years in the wilderness, waiting expectantly for a hopeful future in an abundantly fruitful Promised Land, flowing with milk and honey.[2] The Old Testament prophets longingly looked to a time of restoration and redemption. They anticipated an age of glorious human flourishing when the one true God would reign as their sovereign King and good Shepherd. Anchoring their hope in the bedrock promises of God to his covenant people, the prophets spoke of a future day of great fruitfulness and human flourishing (see for example Is 27:6; Hos 14:4-7).

The human fruitfulness Jesus has in mind during the Upper Room Discourse not only looks back on the prophetic past but also to the future day when he will make all things new. The King of kings has come. His kingdom has arrived on earth. And one day it will come in its fullness. The Gospel writer John expands on Jesus' hopeful teaching concerning human fruitfulness in his inspired vision of Jesus, known as the book of Revelation. There, John paints a glorious image of the fruitfulness that once flowed from Eden filling the new city of Jerusalem. He also writes that the fruitful nations will bring their honor and glory to the new city. The sinless new Jerusalem is presented as a place vibrant with human fruitfulness. John's portrayal of this fruitful abundance is expressed in eschatological language: "Through the middle of the street of the city; also, on either side of the river, [stood] the tree of life with its twelve kinds of fruit, yielding its fruit each month. The leaves of the tree were for the healing of the nations" (Rev 22:2).

When Jesus spoke of fruitfulness in the upper room, he affirmed that redemptive history was anchored in him and moving toward a glorious goal in the new heavens and new earth. Jesus also knew that a time of final judgment awaited fallen humanity and the broken world. The theme of future judgment on human rebellion, faithlessness, and fruitlessness also emerges in Jesus' words to his disciples in the Upper Room Discourse. His comments are indeed sobering. "If anyone does not abide in me he is thrown away like a branch and withers; and the branches are gathered, thrown into the fire, and burned" (Jn 15:6). The apostle Paul echoes our Lord's teaching, "Each one's work will become manifest, for the Day will disclose it, because it will be revealed by fire, and the fire will test what sort of work each one has done" (1 Cor 3:13).

From original creation to final consummation, human fruitfulness is not only an important biblical theme—it is a serious mandate. We are reminded by Jesus in John's Gospel that fruitfulness really matters. A faithful life is a fruitful life. Jesus' invitation to his disciples to abide in him and thereby live a fruitful life is an invitation to each one of us as well. But how are we to understand fruitfulness and human flourishing? What is fruitfulness all about? What are the manifestations of fruitfulness?

MANIFESTATIONS OF FRUITFULNESS

The fruitfulness of intimacy. First, the fruitful life is a flourishing relational life. As image bearers of the trinitarian God, we were not only created with work in mind but also relational intimacy in mind. The Greek word the apostle John repeatedly uses in the Upper Room Discourse that is translated as "abide" or "remain" brings with it the idea of an enduring personal communion.[3] The fruitful life Jesus invites his disciples to experience flows from an intimate relationship with him, continually nurtured by faith-fueled obedience. Jesus makes the connection between the level of our obedience to him and the depth of our intimacy with him when he declares, "Whoever has my commandments and keeps them, he it is who loves me. And he who loves me will be loved by my Father, and I will love him and manifest myself to him" (Jn 14:21).

For Jesus to frame the fruitful life first in terms of relational intimacy should not be surprising. The Hebrew Scriptures consistently present knowing as a relational construct and not merely as an informational construct. To truly know is not only to know something but also to know someone.[4] We quickly grasp the difference when we reflect on our own relationships. There are many acquaintances we know about, but few people we really know up close and personal. There is a big difference between someone saying they know my wife and how I know her. We can know lots of facts about someone—where they were born, what career they have pursued, and how they like to have fun. While these facts may tell us a good deal about a person, they are not the way we truly abide with another at an experiential level. True abiding is primarily not about gaining greater information but about growing in deeper experiential intimacy.

As a pastor I regularly have the privilege of participating in the celebration of life services for those who have died. One of the telling manifestations of a life well lived is not only the individual's quality of character or the worthy accomplishments they might have attained, but also the depth of the relationships they enjoyed. This is not only evidenced in the number of family and friends who gather to remember the person, but also in the tributes shared. I am always amazed how tributes for the deceased speak most about the relational intimacy once enjoyed and now so greatly missed.

A truly fruitful life is manifested in relational intimacy with others and finds its rich source in personal intimacy with Christ. The fruitfulness of a growing intimacy with Jesus is one of the most joyful and telling evidences of the supernatural work of God in our lives. In the Upper Room Discourse, Jesus emphasizes that abiding in his love produces great joy. A growing intimacy with Jesus brings with it a constant awareness that no matter the pains of our past or the pressures of our present, no matter our doubts, our hurts, or our deep disappointments, we're never alone. The encouraging words of Matt Maher's song "Abide with Me" speak eloquently of the constant presence of our Lord.

Abide with me, abide with me.
Don't let me fall, and don't let go.
Walk with me and never leave.
Ever close, God abide with me.[5]

Likewise, the hymn writer C. Austin Miles also captures the flourishing life of fruitful intimacy with Jesus.

And He walks with me, and He talks with me,
And He tells me I am His own,
And the joy we share as we tarry there,
None other has ever known.[6]

A fruitful life is one rich in close relationships with God as well as others.

The fruitfulness of character. A fruitful life is also an increasingly Christlike life. The Holy Scripture speaks of human fruitfulness not only in the context of relational intimacy but also in the formation of Christlike character. The apostle Paul uses the word *fruit* to describe the inner character transformation experienced by apprentices of Jesus through the power of the Holy Spirit: "The fruit of the Spirit is love, joy, peace, patience, kindness, goodness, faithfulness, gentleness, self control" (Gal 5:22-23).

Human fruitfulness is manifested in the kind of people we are becoming, because our inward character transformation profoundly influences the fruitfulness we produce outwardly. True character transformation brings true neighborly love, and it requires a supernatural source. This supernatural source is outwardly expressed with the consistent and compassionate qualities of joy, peace, patience, kindness, goodness, faithfulness, gentleness, and self-control. In order to experience ever increasing Christlike character and to love our neighbor rightly, we must be empowered on a daily basis in a very supernatural way. Neighborly love, rightly understood, must look to and depend on a supernatural source from which to draw proper attitudes and willful actions.

It is not hard to imagine how Christlike character and the moral ecology that flows from it would lead to a more vibrant and just economic system, regardless of how the system is structured. Economic systems depend on virtuous people, because the systems themselves take on a moral aspect from their participants.[7] Virtuous people make virtuous economies. The spiritual formation of a more virtuous people is an important task that the local church is uniquely empowered and positioned to accomplish. The local church, then, is not a neutral or even a parasitic actor within a symbiotic economic system, but rather a prime value-added contributor to flourishing economic and social life. We must see that social capital and economic capital are intrinsically and inextricably linked in a dynamic synergy.

Dallas Willard rightly reminds the church of the pervasive influence that followers of Jesus who display the fruit of the Spirit have in all dimensions of public life.

> A life structured around and animated by the fruits of the Spirit will be one in which personal relationships, which are central to human well-being, are strong and beneficial to everyone involved. . . . Just a moment of reflection will illuminate that the well-being and flourishing such leaders would promote for others in the natural course of living their lives would dramatically influence the social, economic, and governmental arrangements they are involved in or lead.[8]

The kind of people we are becoming and the kind of faith communities we are fostering matters to God and to the world. The book of Proverbs reminds us that "when it goes well with the righteous, the city rejoices" (Prov 11:10). One reason is that even the city's most vulnerable citizens flourish in the midst of a virtuous and robust economy. Such cities also rejoice because the salt and light qualities Christ-followers bring to the marketplace reinforce a strong work ethic and enhance innovation, creativity, and cooperation, which has significant economic implications for human flourishing and the common good. Good work performed in public by Spirit-empowered Christ-followers not only points to gospel plausibility but also brings blessing to the entire community.

The Holy Spirit's guidance, wisdom, and empowerment in this task are essential. We must cease from understanding the Holy Spirit's direction merely in the context of a privatized faith or restricted to the nurturing domain of a local faith community, but rather as enabling us to love our neighbor as we live and work fruitfully in the world. The Holy Spirit empowers us not only for worship on Sunday but also for our work on Monday. As we walk in the Spirit, we work in the Spirit and contribute to the moral, social, and economic goodness of our communities by loving our neighbors in the dynamics of virtuous economic exchange.

The fruitfulness of contribution. A life of fruitfulness is not only manifested in a growing intimacy with Christ and increasing Christlike character, but also by productive contribution to the world. The cultural mandate of Genesis 1 and the human job description given to Adam in Genesis 2 remind us that God designed us to be not only relational beings but productive persons as well (Gen 1:28; 2:15). The call to productivity is made clear in God's covenant with Abraham. When Abraham reached the ripe age of ninety-nine, God invited him to experience a fruitful life of intimacy, character, and contribution.[9] At that time, Abraham was given his new name and promised exceeding fruitfulness, both of procreativity and productivity.[10]

A FRUITFUL LIFE IS A PRODUCTIVE LIFE

Throughout Holy Scripture, a fruitful life is presented as a productive life. One of the constant evidences of true wisdom in the book of Proverbs is diligence and productivity (see Prov 10:4; 12:11; 13:4; 14:14, 23; 21:5). Productive fruitfulness was so important to the psalmist that he cried out with prayerful passion and expectation on behalf of God's covenant people, "Establish the work of our hands, . . . yes establish the work of our hands" (Ps 90:17). Jesus, in one of his most compelling parables, tells the story of three money managers called to productive stewardship. Two productive money managers, who faithfully invested the owner's wealth, are rewarded greatly with more productive opportunities. However, the one unproductive manager is severely rebuked with the gravest consequences in the present and in the future

(Mt 25:14-30). Likewise, the apostle Paul sets a personal example of productivity through his own tent making, which had economic implications for himself and others. He also urges Jesus' followers to be diligent in their work at various points in the epistles (see Col 3:23; 1 Thess 4:9-11; 2 Thess 3:10-12).

Paul's writing on fruitful productivity had a remarkable effect on one of the most productive pastors in history. The letter to the church at Ephesus powerfully shaped the theological understanding and vocational determination of Puritan theologian Richard Baxter, who J. I. Packer once dubbed "the most voluminous English theologian of all time."[11] During his lifetime, Baxter produced nearly ten million written words of apologetics, theological discourse, devotional material, and sermons. This remarkable productivity was fueled by Baxter's reading of Ephesians, which undergirded his conviction that redeemed people were to commit themselves to the task of "redeeming time." Baxter asserted, "To redeem time is to see that we cast none of it away in vain; but use every minute of it as a most precious thing, and spend it wholly in the way of duty."[12] For Baxter, Ephesians 2:10, which speaks clearly to the reality that humans were created with work to do, and Ephesians 5:15-16, which encourages disciplined living and diligent effort, together demonstrate that fruitful productivity is essential to Christian discipleship.

PRODUCTIVITY AND NEIGHBORLY LOVE

We honor God in and through our productive work. As participants within an economic system, we also contribute to others and exhibit neighborly love by creating and adding value through our work. The common good we are called to foster inevitably includes the production and distribution of many common goods and services that enrich others' lives. This idea is captured in the rich, old word *commonwealth*, which is derived from the archaic *commonweal* and demonstrates linguistically that material production and contribution through economic activity bring well-being, safety, and overall happiness to all people in a community. We must grasp with mind and heart the importance of our fruitfulness and productivity as a posture of neighborly love in the public realm. Gene Veith puts it well, "I serve you with my talents, and you serve me with your talents. The result is a divine division of labor in which everyone is constantly giving and receiving in a vast interchange, a unity of diverse people in a social order whose substance and energy is love."[13]

No matter what our vocational calling is, whether our work is paid or not, our contribution of productivity is a vital manifestation of the flourishing, fruitful life from which we serve and love others. Our fruitful productivity within a collaborative economic system fosters vibrant, flourishing communities and cities. The prophet Jeremiah instructs those exiled in the city of Babylon to engage in economic activity that will be beneficial not only to themselves but to all Babylonians. The patriarch Joseph faced the most egregious injustice imaginable from his family as well as from Potiphar's wife. Still, when Joseph was promoted into a place of influence in Egypt, his wise and productive work saved a nation and his people from starvation. The fruitfulness in all dimensions of Joseph's life is highlighted as he names his second son Ephraim, which carries the idea of fruitfulness. With rapturous and joyful praise, Joseph declares the importance of naming his son Ephraim, "For God has made me fruitful in the land of my affliction" (Gen 41:52).

As we begin to grasp the rich theological thread of fruitfulness given to us throughout the pages of Holy Scripture, we see that fruitful productivity and the material wealth that many times flows from it are good things to be pursued and stewarded, not evils to be avoided or distrusted.[14] We also grow in our ability to discern distorted and impoverished understandings of fruitfulness in our own time. In my reflection, three common distortions have emerged in contemporary conversations: success distortion, mediocrity distortion, and pietistic distortion.

Success distortion. The first common distortion of fruitfulness is the success distortion. Through this distorted lens, the truly fruitful life presented in Scripture is co-opted by the cultural narrative of success manifested in material or quantifiable terms. Measures of success like prestige, visibility, fame, power, market share, and monetary accumulation are looked to as the primary manifestations of a fruitful life or a fruitful organization. In the nonprofit context, and particularly the church and parachurch world, it is very common to interpret quantitative growth in money or size as a marker of fruitfulness. All too often the larger a nonprofit organization or church is in terms of attendance, budget, or buildings, the quicker we are to conclude that it must be a fruitful work. We often describe this type of organization as "blessed." The faster the quantifiable growth occurs or the more impressive the story of external success is, the more we tend to flock to the epicenter of success, hoping to learn the secret sauce. Whether we like to admit it or not, we tend to convince ourselves bigger is better and that quantifiable success is a sterling indicator of effectiveness or true fruitfulness.

While quantitative growth can be an indicator of a fruitful work, it can also be evidence of a toxic environment that is anything but fruitful and God-honoring. Quantifiable external indicators of increasing numbers or trend lines may or may not be manifestations of an individual or organization's true health and fruitfulness.

In assessing fruitfulness we must also take into consideration other nonquantifiable factors. For example, we must recognize that fruitfulness often occurs in seasons (see Ps 1). The success distortion often overlooks how the manifestation of Christlike character and the quality of vocational contribution tend to ebb and flow both in the human life cycle and in an organization's life cycle. Tragically, many individuals and organizations live under the ever-present dark shadow of perceived failure simply because they have not experienced impressive, meteoric growth or other quantifiable measures of success.

Jesus' teaching on fruitfulness helps us to see through the success distortion. We are freshly reminded in Jesus' parable of the soils that good soil produces differing amounts of fruitfulness. When the seed fell on good soil it produced grain, "some a hundredfold, some sixty, some thirty" (Mt 13:8). Jesus' parable of the talents also tells us that each money manager was given a differing amount of wealth to invest. Two of the money managers made an equivalent return on the differing amounts entrusted to them to invest wisely. Though the fruitfulness of their faithful work differs in quantifiable terms, both money managers received the very same enthusiastic commendation by the owner, "Well done, good and faithful servant. You have been faithful over a little; I will set you over much. . . . Enter into the joy of your master" (Mt 25:21, 23). When human fruitfulness is measured through a distorted success lens, pride inevitably emerges on the heels of quantifiable success achieved. On the other hand, when quantifiable success is absent, discouragement and despair are sure to follow. Success distortion is perilous both to organizational health and to the individual human soul.

Mediocrity distortion. On the flip side of the success distortion is the mediocrity distortion, where external, quantifiable measures of fruitfulness are not merely dismissed but at times deemed inherently unspiritual. Lack of active work or lack of quantifiable success is heralded as being indicative of spiritual health. But this is hardly the case. On an individual level, a lack of fruitfulness in intimacy, character, or contribution in one's life might actually be a sober marker of spiritual immaturity, spiritual malformation, or stunted spiritual growth. Likewise, a marked lack of the fruitfulness of productivity in one's vocational callings could also be reflective of well-ingrained habits of slothfulness, indiscipline, poor time management, or unwise stewardship.

Nonprofit organizations and churches can buy into the mediocrity distortion of fruitfulness by spiritualizing or making innumerable excuses as to their ongoing culture of mediocrity, inept leadership, and poor outcomes. Underlying a thin veneer of an anemic spirituality often lurks organizational inefficiency, rampant incompetency, and a lack of accountability. The mediocrity distortion also evidences itself in an institutional reluctance to apply quantitative and qualitative assessment tools in order to monitor and advance organizational health and mission advancement. All too often, the spiritually sounding mantra of "just being faithful" masks an underlying dismissal of the vital importance of fruitfulness. Of course being faithful matters, but so does bearing much fruit. A truly faithful life or a truly faithful organization will be a fruitful one.

Pietistic distortion. A third common distortion of the biblical picture of fruitfulness is the pietistic distortion. The pietistic distortion focuses on the personal, privatized, inward, and nonmaterial aspects of human fruitfulness. The pietistic distortion minimizes the goodness and importance of the material world, confining fruitfulness to the spiritual and ethereal realms of human existence. This is not to say that seeing human fruitfulness through a pietistic lens is completely out of focus. Fruitfulness is certainly manifested as one actively nurtures a growing intimate relationship with God and others. And fruitfulness is indeed about experiencing the transformational fruit of the Spirit both as individuals and as a faith community. Fruitfulness flows from our evangelistic efforts to bring others to a saving knowledge of Christ. Yet we are unwise to reduce the full richness of what Jesus had in mind for human flourishing and fruitfulness when we limit his commission to bear much fruit to spiritual activities only.

AFFIRMING THE GOODNESS OF FRUITFULNESS

Pastor Tim Keller founded Redeemer Presbyterian Church in New York City with a strong conviction that the gospel profoundly transforms all dimensions of human existence and leads to human flourishing. Redeemer Presbyterian Church's gospel-centered approach to faith, work, and economic integration has been in many ways a leader in local church innovation. Redeemer's Center for Faith and Work includes an entrepreneurship and innovation program that seeks to develop entrepreneurial leaders as well as investors who are committed to seeking the flourishing of the city.

The Center offers a faith and entrepreneurship course, as well as an entrepreneurship intensive. Most exciting is the Startup Pitch Night designed to celebrate entrepreneurship and promote innovative for-profit businesses and nonprofit initiatives. A five-minute presentation by an entrepreneur is given to a live audience along with a panel of judges. Up to $7,500 can be awarded to an aspiring entrepreneur for his or her startup enterprise. This initiative, and others like it across the country, recognizes the goodness of fruitfulness and affirms it within the church community.

Jesus does emphasize the spiritual fruitfulness and faithfulness of those who are apprenticed to him, who are filled with the Holy Spirit, and who are sharing his good news with others, but this is not the entirety of what Jesus has in mind. When Jesus speaks of a fruitful human life, he points back to our creation design and to the totality of human flourishing. Jesus came not only to save our souls but also to redeem a broken creation and all aspects of human life. Jesus desires to produce the fruit of intimacy, character, *and* productive contribution in the lives of all who follow him. While the evil one seeks to steal, kill, and destroy human flourishing, Jesus came that we may have life and have it abundantly—both now and for all eternity (Jn 10:10).

Abiding and abundant living mean fruitful flourishing. Fruitful flourishing means we are able to love our neighbor with increasing compassion and capacity. If we desire to be faithful, we need to cultivate fruitfulness.

This kind of fruitful life is manifested not only in loving our neighbor well but also in loving our neighborhood well. Not only do our neighbors matter, but neighborhoods matter too.

5

LOVING THE NEIGHBORHOOD

*From the corridors of public power to the halls of
academic innovation, the influence and impact of Mutuality can
be felt everywhere and has the potential to effect change
across the boardrooms and borders everywhere.*

STEPHEN M. BADGER II, "EXPLORING MUTUALITY"

*Then the LORD God said, "It is not good that man should be alone;
I will make him a helper fit for him."*

GENESIS 2:18

I like cars. But I should be clear: my affection for cars is not so much about their cool factor as their reliability factor. First and foremost I want an automobile that is going to get me where I need to go without breaking down along the way. When I drive to work in the morning, I'm grateful for reliable transportation. But seldom do I even consider all the neighborly love it took for me to get where I need to go.

Many people played a role. Getting me to work every day requires national and global neighbors. It starts with those who mined the raw materials my car was constructed from. Other neighbors transported the raw materials to factories, while others worked diligently to ensure that the factory had electrical power to operate. Many of my global neighbors, who I have never met and most likely never will meet, designed my car for reliability, comfort, and convenience. Other neighbors worked with skillful precision along with robots to assemble my automobile. Truck drivers, ship captains, dockworkers, and railroad personnel transported my car to the auto dealership in my community.

When I made the big step to purchase a car, other neighbors serviced it, a banking agent financed it, and a Kansas worker from the Department of Motor Vehicles validated my property rights, collected sales tax, and licensed the vehicle to me. Neighbors who work at the gas station I frequent make it possible for me to quickly and conveniently obtain the fuel that is necessary to keep my car going. If I run into a problem or need maintenance for my car, I head to the reliable auto repair shop just down the street, where highly skilled mechanics use modern computer technology to evaluate my car and repair it quickly.

Whether or not we need a car to get to work each morning, it is all too easy for us to forget the myriad of people who make this convenient and dependable mode of transportation happen in our global neighborhood. Every day, it takes a global village to get me to work on time.

Whether it is the car we drive or the cell phone we use, the pen in our pocket or the shoes we wear, it takes a lot of people around the world to keep us going. Yet seldom do we pause to contemplate the collaborative economic web we count on every day. Most of us take for granted global currency valuations, government monetary policies, and price mechanisms that guide the innumerable economic decisions made by billions of people across the globe. Many who work in government and nonprofit sectors fail to consider that the private sector and its powerful economic engine make possible their paycheck. Modern economic life and its interconnected market forces enable neighborly love to be expressed to the billions of God's image bearers who currently grace our planet—from Kansas City to Beijing. When you consider this process, it can take your breath away.

While such a vast web of economic collaboration may amaze us, we should not be totally surprised. This mutuality of human collaboration within an economic ecosystem reflects God's creation design. The Bible tells us we were created to work together, cultivating blessings from the created order and expressing neighborly love in and through the collaborative work we do every day. This reality should cause us to reconsider what Jesus desires as he calls us to love our neighbor as we love ourselves. It seems as though he might desire more than extending a helping hand to a next-door neighbor in need.

THE FIRST NEIGHBORHOOD

If we are going to grasp God's design for vibrant neighborhoods, we would be wise to take a closer look at the first neighborhood described in Genesis 2, where we catch a glimpse of the Eden neighborhood. While Genesis 1 looks at original creation with a wide-angle literary lens, offering a panorama view of creation, chapter two zooms in, offering a narrower focus on humanity's place within the created order. We see that God designed humanity with a neighborhood in mind. Let's take a closer look.

These are the generations
of the heavens and the earth when they were created,
in the day that the Lord God made the earth and the heavens.

When no bush of the field was yet in the land and no small plant of the field had yet sprung up—for the Lord God had not caused it to rain on the land, and there was no man to work the ground, and a mist was going up from the land and was watering the whole face of the ground—then the LORD God formed the man of dust from the ground and breathed into his nostrils the breath of life, and the man became a living creature. And the LORD God planted a garden in Eden, in the east, and there he put the man whom he had formed. (Gen 2:4-8)

A place of productive work. The first neighborhood was a beautiful place of fruitful and productive work. Like any good city planner, Creator God knew what resources were needed for his beautifully designed neighborhood to flourish. Yet as the master architect, God recognized incompleteness that needed further completion. The Genesis writer emphasizes that initially there were *no plants*, *no rain*, and *no human beings* in God's creation. Seeing this, God continues shaping and creating within his creation masterpiece, bringing about order and completeness. God creates Adam, plants a garden, and puts Adam in that garden. Integral to God's creation design is a closely knit interdependent ecosystem where vibrant human productivity takes place. In Genesis 2, we listen as God gives Adam a more specific twofold job description that gives specificity to the cultural mandate issued in Genesis 1. The text reads, "The LORD God took the man and put him in the garden of Eden to work it and keep it" (Gen 2:15).

Adam's twofold job description is captured in the two phrases "to work it" and "to keep it." As an image bearer of God, Adam was given a unique capacity and calling within the created order to cultivate and protect the Eden neighborhood. The Hebrew word ʿăbōdâ in Genesis 2, translated "to work," is used in the Old Testament to describe a variety of human work, from priests offering sacrifices in the tabernacle to farmers working in the field to craftsmen building things. This word ʿăbōdâ is also used to describe humans worshiping God.[1] It is important to grasp that God designed the work we do and the worship we do to be a seamless reality in our daily lives. Each day we are invited to embrace a sacred dance of joyful intimacy and creative productivity in a God-bathed world. We don't worship our work—that is idolatry. But from the beginning our work was designed to be a primary way we worship God. In the first neighborhood there was no separation between Adam's work and Adam's worship. There was no gap between Sunday worship and Monday work. For Adam, work was a vital aspect of prayerful intimacy with his Creator, and prayerful intimacy with his Creator was a vital aspect of his work.

A place of productive collaboration. Adam was created with work and productivity in mind, but he was also created with community in mind. When we arrive at Genesis 2:18, we experience a kind of dissonant chalkboard moment in the biblical narrative. Growing up, one of my high school history teachers had the obnoxious habit of screeching chalk across the blackboard. With such a hideous sound, any student taking a brief snooze during the lecture was suddenly aroused from slumber. Our teacher's chalkboard moments got our attention.

In a similar manner, the Genesis writer uses dissonance to alert us that something demands our attention. After God repeatedly says in chapter one that creation is good, in chapter two we hear the triune God say something is not good. Specifically, God says, "It is not good that the man should be alone" (Gen 2:18). To be clear, God is not saying oops, as if he made a mistake. However, we do hear a seeming dissonance, a kind of creation chalkboard moment. There is some sort of incompleteness needing completion.

At first blush this dissonant chalkboard moment doesn't seem to make sense. In Genesis 2 we are introduced to sinless Adam, who lives in a pristine, sinless neighborhood in perfect communion with God. How on earth could something be "not good" in that picture? Nevertheless, the text makes clear that it is not good that Adam is alone? Why? We could conjecture why Adam being alone was deemed not good. Perhaps Adam's triune Creator believed it was not good that Adam, his image bearer, could not experience the kind of intimacy and love that God experienced within the Trinity. This is a common way of understanding this divine assertion. However, the Creator's solution in the text offers another important insight that sheds light on why Adam's aloneness is not good. Simply put, Adam could not accomplish on his own the big job given to humanity.

A HELPER FOR WHAT?

God responds to the not-goodness of Adam's aloneness by stating, "I will make him a helper fit for him" (Gen 2:18). Eve is created as Adam's helper, but a helper for what? It should be noted that the Hebrew word translated *helper* is not a degrading word in any sense.[2] The Genesis writer is describing an equal and complementary partner for Adam. Let's recall that in Genesis 1 the cultural mandate for human fruitfulness is about both procreativity and productivity. While Eve's creation will make possible the fruitfulness of human procreativity, Eve's creation will also make possible the fruitfulness of human productivity.

The unfolding narrative in Genesis 2 clearly and repeatedly emphasizes human productivity. Human procreativity and marriage do not get featured until the very end of the chapter. Adam alone could not fulfill the job description given to him to cultivate and keep the Eden neighborhood. Nor could Adam alone carry out this task in the much bigger garden.

God ultimately intended to share with his creation. From the beginning, human work was designed for mutual collaboration.

So who will work with Adam? As Genesis 2 unfolds, God parades in front of Adam the many animals he's made. Adam exercises his rightful dominion by naming them, but God also has something else up his creative and sovereign sleeve. By parading the animals in front of Adam, God prepares Adam to see the uniqueness of Eve as his fellow image bearer and co-laborer. Adam knows the animals can't do human work and fulfill the vast human job description to cultivate and protect the planet. Only another who bears God's image can do this. Our English word *collaboration* has co-laboring inherent within it. When we collaborate, we work together toward a good outcome that benefits others. As Genesis 2 builds to its creation crescendo, it is important for us to see Adam and Eve are not only the first marital couple, they are also the first workplace dream team, brought together by God to add value to the Eden neighborhood. When Eve comes on the scene, the first human economy is created.

THE FIRST ECONOMY

When we take a closer look, we see that the thrust of the Genesis 2 narrative is not merely about humans having babies but rather about humans doing collaborative work. When God forms Eve, he creates a collaborative economic ecosystem within the Eden neighborhood. We must grasp with heart and mind that economics, properly understood, is not a complex, modern academic discipline divorced from theological reflection. Instead, economic collaboration is a vital part of God's creation design for human flourishing. If we care about maintaining biblical fidelity, as well as cultivating human flourishing, then economics matters.

It is helpful to note that we get our English word *economics* from a combination of two Greek words: *oikos* and *nomia*. When these Greek words come together, we have *oikonomia*, which means "household stewardship."[3] It is not insignificant that throughout the pages of inspired Holy Scripture the strong and prominent threads of households and stewardship regularly appear in the tapestry of human flourishing.

Economics can be and is defined in many ways, but one writer echoes Genesis 2 as he describes economics as "the care for our common home; or the art of living together."[4] How differently would we think about the important and complex reality of modern economics if we first saw it as the stewardship we all have been given by God for *caring for our common home and cultivating the art of living together*? Would we not look at economics differently and value economics more if we saw economic interaction as the place where value is created and where collaborative neighborly love is exchanged? How important might greater economic reflection be in the late modern world, where humans who see the world so differently need to learn to live together in our interconnected global village, in light of those differences?[5]

HUMAN FLOURISHING AND ECONOMIC FLOURISHING

When we take a closer look at Genesis 2, we see how family and work come together as basic components of God's design for a flourishing economy. Both procreativity and productivity are woven into the seamless fabric of the cultural mandate for human flourishing and fruitfulness. When we look deeper into so many broken neighborhoods in our cities, we often see the breakdown of the family. Economic research indicates the number one empirical factor for material poverty is relational poverty specifically evidenced in out-of-wedlock births.[6] In addition to the breakdown of marriage and family life, we also must see the brokenness of neighborhoods through the lens of the breakdown of economic life.

I was reminded of this truth in the aftermath of great rioting in Baltimore. Speaking of the dire need for change, an urban leader called not primarily for more government intervention but for members of the Baltimore private sector to work diligently in job creation and economic renewal.

The simplest, most direct way to offer hope to discouraged people is to hire them. The Baltimore business community has a simple message to law enforcement and elected officials: "Help us help you." People making good wages, working at jobs they are proud of, don't destroy themselves or the place where they live. We have the political and business talent to rebuild one of American's great cities, once we focus on creating the conditions for job growth.[7]

We must grasp with both mind and heart that human flourishing and economic flourishing go hand in hand. Good neighbors make good neighborhoods, and good neighborhoods make good neighbors. Of course, in today's globalized world of a modern economy, there is a much greater diversity and complexity than in the first neighborhood. But God's design for the goodness of work collaboration remains.

ECONOMICS AND THE PROBLEM OF SIN

Economic life is messy and imperfect because we live in the context of broken neighbors and broken neighborhoods. While this pains us, it should not surprise us. Genesis 2 is a picture of our entrepreneurial God who sovereignly launches an enterprise with risk. God doesn't hold humanity's hand, but instead gives Adam and Eve a job description alongside of the raw material to work with and says, "Now get to work and get to work together." God designed the perfect neighborhood where intimacy of relationships, individual contribution, and mutual collaboration flourished. But something tragic happened. Humankind committed an unthinkable rebellion against God. Sin and death invaded the garden. Corruption and vandalism of God's design took place in horrific ways. In Eden it was no longer a beautiful day in the neighborhood, nor was it a beautiful day for a neighbor.

In Genesis 3 we observe one of the dire consequences of the curse of sin on human procreativity and productivity. Pain becomes an unwelcomed companion to every childbirth. Work becomes toilsome and difficult. Thorns and thistles plague the ground. Instead of being fulfilling, a great deal of human work is now dehumanizing. Conflict emerges. Inevitably, frustrating employees and demanding bosses must be dealt with. Strife, struggle, and conflict will emerge in the office and the factory. While work remains meaningful and important, the humans who engage it will feel more like they're in war zones than work zones. Work in the neighborhood is broken.

No matter where we live or what we do, we all live and work in a broken neighborhood. No matter how pedicured our lawns or progressive our schools, every neighborhood is badly broken at its core. Neighborly love expressed through our economic collaboration often fails us. I was reminded of the brokenness of my suburban neighborhood when my wife, Liz, and I contracted to have windows replaced on our home. The contractors told us there might be more work to do when they pulled out our old windows. As the skilled workers removed our existing windows, Liz and I held our breath. Sure enough, hidden behind the exterior walls were water damage and faulty construction from when the home was first built twenty years ago. The construction workers, who we had depended on to build our house, had failed us. A good deal of the front of our house had to be repaired and replaced. What hurt most was the high economic price we paid for workers who many years before had cut economic corners to maximize their profit. A lack of neighborly love led to shoddy work.

We live and work in a fallen economic world. The harmonious collaborative work God designed us to do is now a target of

Satan's fury and destruction. In a world of satanic influence, where sinful human brokenness and systemic injustices color economic exchange, and in a world where humans possess a seemingly infinite number of desires, economic systems seek ways to efficiently exchange things and allocate resources that are finite. This is the heart of economics. Indeed, economist Thomas Sowell defines economics as "the allocation of scarce resources with alternate uses."[8] Sowell's definition is helpful even for non-economists. The difficult work of economics is to determine how best to navigate the complex relationship between the resources that are available and the infinite (and at times sinful) human desires that we each experience.

While there is certainly no perfect economic system, I am persuaded that the free-market economic system we currently have is the best system for economic behavior and exchange because it allows for proper self-interest, responsibility, incentive, and human collaboration. This is not to say that our free-market systems are above critique or criticism. To function properly and responsibly, free markets require governmental oversight and enforcement of property rights and contracts. There must also be mechanisms for preventing and addressing fraud. In our modern times the free market has been very effective in lifting millions of people out of poverty, raising standards of living, and encouraging technological innovation, even as it has led to growing economic inequality for many and at times has not stewarded the environment with proper care and diligence.[9]

Though it can at times allow excesses and abuse, theologian Scott Rae affirms the free-market approach, offering this helpful perspective:

> Economic systems that enlarge the freedom of human beings
> to exercise their entrepreneurial traits, cooperate in using

their gifts, support their households, and personally care for the poor are closer to the biblical ideal than those that inhibit these activities. . . . Market-oriented economics provide the best means for the most people to achieve self-support.[10]

As we engage economic systems with a theological perspective, we must use wisdom and discernment. We must not be drawn into an unbiblical scarcity mentality that looks at what exists and says "this is all there is." And we must not minimize the dynamic and seemingly unlimited number of human wants and desires. Those desires are real and many times are attempting to meet very legitimate human needs, albeit in sometimes illegitimate or ill-advised ways. Rather, we must recognize that economic systems allow us to create and add value in the world, while also making it possible for us to allocate finite resources through monetized price mechanisms. In our market-oriented economy, supply and demand as well as price mechanisms help us allocate and distribute goods and services.

For example, I may want to enjoy an expensive steak on the grill each night or to boil a tasty Maine lobster. But if I, alongside my many national and global neighbors, were able to indulge that desire every day, there simply would not be enough steak or lobster to go around. This is where price mechanisms aid the distribution of limited resources. And in most instances, this mechanism works with remarkable effectiveness. Even so, sin succeeds in finding toxic ways to destroy, devalue, and dehumanize within our economic system.

I think of economic systems kind of like police officers, who direct traffic in busy intersections so that there are fewer crashes. Certainly, these officers cannot prevent every calamity. Despite their presence, crashes still sometimes occur and require attention and intervention. Yet by and large, people who are given both opportunity and responsibility to get what they need and to go where they need to go without undue interference do so in an orderly manner.

In today's modern economies built-in incentives shape the allocation of resources by determining how things and services are to be priced. Across the globe we use various forms of what we call money to exchange value with others. Certainly economics is a very complex discipline, but at its core it is about a vast interconnected and interdependent web of collaboration, where we express neighborly love by honoring, serving, and adding value to others—whether that neighbor lives next door or thousands of miles away in China.

LOVING OUR BROKEN NEIGHBORHOODS

So why should we love our broken neighborhoods? Why should we care about others' economic well-being and not just focus on our own self-fulfillment and economic advancement? Because God still loves his broken world. Jesus loved a broken neighborhood so much he moved into it. The Gospel writer John speaks of Jesus this way, "The Word became flesh and dwelt among us, and we have seen his glory, glory as of the only Son from the Father, full of grace and truth" (Jn 1:14).

Jesus now beckons us to follow him, embracing him as Savior and Lord of our lives. As his apprentices, we are called to pursue the common good in the spaces and communities where he has placed us, and to share the good news of Jesus with others. The power of the gospel transforms neighbors and neighborhoods, speaking into every facet of economic life and paving the way for redemptive collaboration with others.

Loving our neighborhoods is not only a vital outworking of the Great Commandment but also a vital part of Jesus' teaching on the Great Commission—to make disciples of all nations, teaching them to obey everything Jesus taught. The Great Commandment and the Great Commission are intertwined and brilliantly put on display in Jesus' Sermon on the Mount, as Jesus calls his apprentices to be salt and light in the world (Mt 5:13-16). One of the primary ways we are salt and light is through the good collaborative work we are called to do every day. As people see our work and the kind of workers we are, as well as the ways we add value to others and how we care for the neighborhood, they will get a powerful glimpse of who Jesus is and why he matters so much to our broken world. In our interconnected global economy, this kind of faithful presence can have a massive impact. Jesus knew the way we work every day has the potential to reveal much about us and the Audience of One we serve. Both our collaborative economic work and our gracious words are gospel witness.

If we are convinced God has called us to love our neighborhoods, how then do we do it? We must begin with a posture of repentance. In one way or another we all contribute to the brokenness of our interconnected world—spiritually, socially, and economically. As part of a free-market economic system, whether we are materially poorer or richer, each of us in some way is complicit both on an individual and systemic basis in not loving our neighbor as we should. Our sinfulness finds a welcome home in our daily economic life.

Some of us bilk the government system by faking disability to get government payments, create questionable tax shelters, or cheat on our taxes. Others may engage in exploitative business practices. We may own or invest in socially irresponsible businesses that extract value from the community instead of adding value to others. We may have financially gained in our investment portfolio from businesses that prey on the poor, like payday loans or real estate investment trusts that shield absent landlords who don't invest back into the community. We may support through our taxes or donations to nonprofit organizations that harm the unborn. We may have an attitude of entitlement that leads us to ignore our responsibility to serve others. Or we may shop away our boredom and anxiety. In both sins of omission and commission, we all need a posture of repentance for not loving our neighbor and not seeking the common good through our economic activity.

TAKING A HOLISTIC APPROACH

It is vital that we look at our broken neighborhoods holistically. We must open our eyes to see both the poverty and the potential of every person—spiritually, relationally, socially, physically, and emotionally. Human flourishing is a multifaceted reality, just as human impoverishment is multifaceted. Stanford economist Raj Chetty has done telling research on the shrinking middle class and the lack of economic mobility for many in our nation. His data points to two primary contributors to this lack of economic flourishing that many experience—bad neighborhoods and bad schools. Chetty also points to helpful government policies, neighborhood churches, and two-parent families as three crucial components that lead to greater community flourishing.[11]

Do we see the vital importance of working for wise government economic policies, reinforcing family life, and supporting local churches? How are we investing in our local church? Are we planting churches in our cities and helping other local churches flourish? How are we building strong marriages and families so that children grow up in a nourishing space with both a mom and a dad? Will we nurture the church and our personal and family relationships, and advocate for those who cannot advocate for themselves?

A holistic view looks beyond a mere materialistic view of the world, which often assumes that allocating money to a problem will solve it. Money does matter, but it is not all that matters.

Economic flourishing is about more than money. Many who have a great deal of economic resources are deeply impoverished. Think of the many Powerball lottery winners whose lives take a downward spiral in the midst of their abundant financial resources.

Taking a holistic approach to loving our neighborhoods begins as we seek to make a difference wherever God has planted us in our vocational callings. Are you living as salt and light in your vocation? Are you doing good work, whether or not that work brings a paycheck or other financial reward? Are you stewarding well your vocational power and influence?[12] Organizational researcher and bestselling author Jim Collins encourages all workers, regardless of their organizational position or power, to create pockets of greatness within their vocational sphere of influence.[13] Work well done not only is highly rewarding, it also has a way of blessing others and promoting the common good.

SEEKING THE COMMON GOOD

The apostle Paul calls Christ-followers and the local church to seek the flourishing of all people. In penning his Spirit-inspired letter to the Galatians, Paul writes, "So then, as we have opportunity, let us do good to everyone, and especially to those who are of the household of faith" (Gal 6:10). One of the most important places where we seek the common good is in our daily work. The prophet Jeremiah called the exiles in Babylon to care for their pagan neighborhood. One of the main ways God's covenant people were to seek the *shalom* or the flourishing of Babylon was to engage in economic activity. Creating economic value and sharing economic value with the Babylonian neighborhood was a vital component of nurturing *shalom*. As Jeremiah exhorts the Jewish exiles to seek the welfare of the city of their captivity, he speaks not only in familial terms but also in economic terms, calling them to build homes and plant gardens (Jer 29:5-7). In the interconnected economic web of a flourishing Babylon, God's covenant people would experience their own economic flourishing. In seeking the common good of the city of Babylon, they too would experience the common good and common goods of mutual economic collaboration.

In the congregation I have the privilege of serving in Kansas City, I regularly get glimpses of Jesus' apprentices faithfully doing their daily work with a heart and eye to loving their neighborhoods and furthering the common good. Bob is one of them. By day, Bob works as a property management director of a publicly traded firm. The company Bob serves has about ten thousand housing units scattered about in eight states. Bob's for-profit company brings its expertise to the free market and collaborates with the nonprofit and government sectors to provide affordable and safe housing to many underresourced families. Bob and his company have experienced a great deal of economic success and personal satisfaction because of their work. As a follower of Jesus, Bob has a heart and eye to the common good. Speaking of his job, Bob says, "I am sure I made some pension fund in Newark happy. But it pales in comparison to driving over to Friendship Village at 56th and Swope and seeing 144 families that have respectable, affordable housing that wouldn't be there today if we hadn't been there."[14]

As a person called by God to the vocation of business, Bob is not only making a profit; he also loves his neighbor well by making a big difference in Kansas City neighborhoods. Bob is seeing his work in a free-market economy through the lens of an economics of mutuality.

PROMOTING AN ECONOMICS OF MUTUALITY

While the free-market economy is the best less-than-perfect system we currently have, one possibility for making the free market better is to move beyond approaches that look to the sole bottom line of profit and to move toward triple bottom-line approaches that take into account not only profit but also promoting the flourishing of people as well as the planet. Yes, profit remains a key bottom line. But people and the planet become bottom lines as well. Supporters of this kind of economics of mutuality are offering a salutary critique of the hyperindividualism and narrow focus of those free-market systems that assert the sole purpose of business is to maximize shareholder profit.[15] One of the thought leaders promoting the adoption of a triple bottom line in business is the Mars Corporation. The Mars company not only makes my life more enjoyable by producing my favorite chocolate snack, peanut M&Ms, but also is paving the way forward for many profitable business enterprises. For the Mars Corporation and other for-profit companies like them, there is an increasing recognition of a more complex bottom line than shareholder value only. Yes, there is a good and needed desire to sustain profitability for the long haul, but not without taking into account the resulting positives and negatives on people and the planet as a whole.

Mars board chairman, Stephen M. Badger II, describes his all-in commitment to a free-market system and his embrace of the economics of mutuality this way: "Clearly, then, mutuality-creating shared value for all stakeholders through a form of capitalism and responsible business practices that defines success in much broader terms than profits for shareholders—has had a profound effect on Mars and indeed my own life."[16] I am hopeful that with business leaders like Stephen Badger, our free-market system can function better for the flourishing of all our neighbors and neighborhoods. The economics of mutuality align well with biblical principles for human flourishing, and suggest good possibilities for enhancing the common good. A corporation is a good thing, but a corporation that has corporate social responsibility not only to its shareholders but also toward its local and global neighborhood is even better.[17]

We all have a part to play in loving our neighborhoods and seeking the common good. From Genesis to Revelation we were designed to work together and to collaborate for the glory of God and the common good. Yet we seek the good of our neighborhoods not with some utopian vision but with a hopeful realism lived out in the messiness of our everyday life. Christ has promised one day to return and to make all wrongs right. We can't bring the new Jerusalem neighborhood to earth by ourselves. Only Jesus can do that. And he will. Jesus has gone away to prepare a place for us, and there is a glorious future day coming when he will bring our new Jerusalem neighborhood with him to the renewed earth. Until then, we are called and commissioned to love our neighbors and our broken neighborhoods as we live the life of Christ in the vast web of economic collaboration in which we work, seeking the flourishing of all as we await his coming. We will need an abundance of economic wisdom if we are to be a faithful presence for our Lord and champions of human flourishing.

6

ECONOMIC WISDOM

*Spokespersons for Christ are under the
overarching imperative to love God and to love
their neighbors as themselves. Their responsibility for
what honors God and what is good for the public as well
as their closer neighbors dictates that they deal with
economic, political, professional, and social issues
that seriously impact life and well-being.*

DALLAS WILLARD, *THE DIVINE CONSPIRACY CONTINUED*

*Give her of the fruit of her hands,
and let her works praise her in the gates.*

PROVERBS 31:31

How does our call to neighborly love find its way forward in the context of a politically polarized nation and in our increasingly connected global world, with its various political philosophies and economic systems? In addition, how do we hold to Christ's robust call to neighborly love in the midst of ever-growing economic complexities like the changing nature of work itself, the development of new robotic technologies, emerging global demographics, and global climate change? In this time of tectonic change and economic displacement, many image bearers of God find themselves ill-equipped to perform the skills employers require. For many, the door to economic opportunity is presently ajar. And for some the door is locked tightly shut.

In this brave new world, neighborly love is needed more than ever. And our neighborly love needs more than good intentions; it needs a great deal of wisdom to guide it. The good news is Holy Scripture offers a great deal of timeless economic wisdom. Neighborly love compels us as followers of Jesus to incarnate this economic wisdom and to share it with our world. Tragically, many Christian leaders have not been faithful to this important stewardship.[1] David Gill rightly throws down the gauntlet for needed change.

> Pastors should teach people about work and economics because it's a theme throughout the Bible, from Genesis to Revelation. That's what I would call the "argument from above." It's a mandate of our faith if we want to be orthodox and biblical, no matter what our tradition is. But the other argument is "the argument from below." People in the workplace need insight. We're desperate, really, for ethical insight, managerial insight, economic insight, and the Bible is full of that type of information and insight. I think that out of sympathy and a desire to help our people out in the workplace and help our country, help our globe, really—we ought to be doing that.[2]

THE WISDOM OF SOLOMON

In our age of excessive noise and overwhelming triviality, we need a fresh and invigorating dose of biblical wisdom to inform, compel, and guide us. The wisdom of Solomon is a good place to start. In biblical history, King Solomon was regarded as a man of great wisdom, yet we tend to forget how he gained his remarkable insight. Following in his father David's imposing shoes must have been a tall order for young Solomon when he ascended the throne. Solomon recognized his human inadequacy and went before the Lord in prayerful worship. God appeared to Solomon in the night and asked the young king what his heart longed for most. Solomon responded, "Give me now wisdom and knowledge to go out and come in before this people, for who can govern this people of yours, which is so great?" (2 Chron 1:10). God granted Solomon's request, honoring his humble and sincere desire to contribute to the flourishing of a nation.

> God answered Solomon, "Because this was in your heart, and you have not asked for possessions, wealth, honor, or the life of those who hate you, and have not even asked for long life, but have asked for wisdom and knowledge for yourself that you may govern my people over whom I have made you king, wisdom and knowledge are granted to you. I will also give you riches, possessions, and honor, such as none of the kings had who were before you, and none after you shall have the like." (2 Chron 1:11-12)

God's gracious gift of knowledge and wisdom was granted to Solomon and had economic implications, not only for Solomon but also for the entire nation. We must not entertain the idea that somehow the nation Solomon led experienced immediate economic vitality. God did not drop material riches and wealth like manna out of the sky. Rather, the wisdom given to Solomon was applied to everyday life by a nation over time, and it began to produce value, bringing with it wealth creation. It is also not insignificant that Solomon presided over a nation located on a strategic strip of land between the two superpowers of Egypt to the south and Assyria to the north. Like the premium property of Boardwalk on a Monopoly board, Solomon operated a lucrative tollbooth through which the vast majority of goods and armies of antiquity flowed. Solomon wisely maximized his strategic location, providing great economic opportunity and wealth capacity-building potential.

Under the providence and sovereignty of God, some of the economic wisdom Solomon employed is preserved for us in Holy Scripture, particularly in the Old Testament book of Proverbs.[3] John Bolt makes a strong case for the rich theological basis on which the book of Proverbs rests. "Along with key theological themes from the Christian doctrines of creation, anthropology, and eschatology, biblical wisdom offers the prudential guidance that we, as free Christian disciples led by the Holy Spirit, can apply to life in our modern economy."[4]

How do we love our neighbor in an increasingly interconnected and interdependent globalized world? Neighborly love calls for the integration of both wise theological insight and sound economic thinking. A closer examination of Proverbs will get us moving in that helpful direction. Three main threads of economic wisdom are woven into the wisdom-laden fabric of Proverbs: economic integrity, economic diligence, and economic generosity.

Economic integrity. The writer of Proverbs makes the case that economic exchange has an essential moral component. It requires virtuous people who act rightly in the proper fear of God and love for neighbor. Any good system of exchange needs virtuous people who promote honesty, transparency, and fairness in their economic activity. In Proverbs, we hear that God delights in honest economic activity. We also hear a denunciation of dishonesty in an economic system that is rigged. "A false balance is an abomination to the LORD, but a just weight is his delight" (Prov 11:1). "The getting of treasures by a lying tongue is a fleeting vapor and a snare of death" (Prov 21:6). Not only are deceptive economic measurements called out as morally wrong, the corruption of bribery is also condemned. "The wicked accepts a bribe in secret to pervert the ways of justice" (Prov 17:23). Wealth obtained by cutting corners and shady economic practices is also condemned. "A ruler who lacks understanding is a cruel oppressor, but he who hates unjust gain will prolong his days" (Prov 28:16).

The economic integrity of any system of exchange is also seen in how discrepancy of economic power is navigated. Improper use of wealth and outright abuse of economic power is abhorred. Proverbs as well as many other biblical texts speak with the strongest language about oppression and exploitation of the economically vulnerable (see Lev 19:33-36). "Whoever oppresses the poor to increase his own wealth, or gives to the rich, will only come to poverty" (Prov 22:16). "Do not rob the poor, because he is poor, or crush the afflicted at the gate" (Prov 22:22). Charging exorbitant interest was particularly exploitative to the most economically vulnerable. "Whoever multiplies his wealth by interest and profit gathers it for him who is generous to the poor" (Prov 28:8). In an agrarian economy, land was inextricably linked to multigenerational family well-being and sustainable economic life. Obtaining the land of the poor through fraudulent means was seen as a vile and immoral economic action. "Do not move the ancient landmark that your fathers have set" (Prov 22:28).

Strong affirmations of the virtue of humility, as well as strong warnings regarding the vice of human pride, are regularly embedded in the wise words of Proverbs. Honesty between actors in an economic exchange is not merely a helpful option. Honesty of transactions is essential to flourishing economic life. Without the virtue of honesty, abuse, corruption, and injustice are assured to enter any economic system. Economist Thomas Sowell puts it well: "In short, honesty is more than a moral principle. It is also a major economic factor. While government can do little to create honesty directly, in various ways it can indirectly either support or undermine the traditions on which honest conduct is based."[5]

The Great Recession. The Great Recession speaks loudly to the lingering consequences of an economic system compromised by less than virtuous people. The Great Recession began in the United States in December 2007 with the bursting of an eight trillion dollar housing bubble. The domino effect of this rupturing of confidence in the financial markets reverberated throughout the world, threatening to bring the largest economy in the world to its knees. From 2007 to 2009, the United States and much of the world faced the strong headwinds of a difficult recessionary period. Governments took bold action, adding massive amounts of liquidity to restore confidence in financial markets. However, the traumatic loss of wealth and resultant level of fear led to sharp cutbacks in capital and consumer spending.

A great deal of commentary and punditry has been offered as to the cause of the Great Recession. While government policy most likely was a contributive factor, a big culprit was the unscrupulous marketing of bundled investments containing high-risk subprime mortgage loans. Risky mortgage loans were made to individuals and families who could not afford the houses they purchased. When these families defaulted on their loans, the entire market crumbled. When the layers of the financial markets were peeled back, and the many individual and corporate players exposed, a common thread emerged. The lack of virtuous and integral persons led to the widespread, shortsighted pursuit of immediate financial gain that sought to game the system at the expense of the common good.

Observing the lingering effects of the Great Recession, it is easy to point self-righteous fingers at government officials and Wall Street firms. However, even the smallest lack of honesty and transparency in our daily economic transactions with others matters a great deal. Who has not had the painful experience of being over-charged for a product or a service? Many have discovered additional fees tacked on to their monthly phone bill, or purchased a junker from a shady used-car salesperson. While having appropriate laws guiding and guarding economic life is important, laws in themselves do not make virtuous actors in economic exchange. For an economy to flourish, virtuous actors must embrace a voluntary compliance to the unenforceable. They must do what is right in the myriad of transactions they engage. Doing what is right cannot be legislatively coerced but rather must be internally guided by a moral compass in the micro-universe of everyday economic interactions. At its core, economic corruption stems from individual moral failure and results in enormous personal and public cost.

Proverbs reminds us that God's design for economic vitality works best in an honest marketplace where the moral compass of virtuous people has a true north setting. The kind of neighbors we are and have matters to the economy. In an interconnected global economy, no one is an economic island. The health and vitality of an economy reflects the integrity or lack of integrity of a people.

Economic diligence. Proverbs not only speaks a great deal about economic integrity, it also emphasizes the wisdom of economic diligence. The wise words of Proverbs are built on the bedrock truth of God's creation design that diligent work is inherent to being human.[6] Productivity and wealth creation are manifestations of wise living, although diligent work does not always lead to prosperity.[7] In Proverbs we are instructed that diligent labor within an economic system is a telling indicator of true wisdom. On the other hand, slothfulness or laziness is an identifiable mark of a person who lacks wisdom and love.

One of the consistent thematic connections made explicit in Proverbs is the close relationship seen between laziness and economic impoverishment. On the flip side, the close relationship between work diligence and economic flourishing is repeatedly affirmed. "Lazy hands make for poverty, but diligent hands bring wealth" (Prov 10:4 NIV). "The plans of the diligent lead to profit as surely as haste leads to poverty" (Prov 21:5 NIV). Throughout Proverbs, sluggards, who are more prone to sleep than to work, are prodded to change their ways.

A little sleep, a little slumber,
    a little folding of the hands to rest—
and poverty will come on you like a thief
    and scarcity like an armed man. (Prov 24:33-34 NIV)

Writing to the church at Thessalonica, the apostle Paul echoes the wisdom of Proverbs as he affirms the essential importance of hard work and economic diligence. Paul speaks forcefully about the peril of idleness. He reminds followers of Jesus in the strongest of words that those who are unwilling to work should not eat (2 Thess 3:10).

Proverbs also explores other aspects of wisdom relating to economic diligence. While hard work and economic diligence are a mark of wise living, work and economic wealth can become idolatrous. Wisdom informs us how foolish it is to look to economic wealth and not to God for human security. Economic gain and all manifestations of material wealth are fickle and fleeting as the wind.

Do not toil to acquire wealth;
    be discerning enough to desist.
When your eyes light on it, it is gone,
    for suddenly it sprouts like wings,
    flying like an eagle toward heaven. (Prov 23:4-5)

Economic success can also deceive us into lax management practices, resulting in the eventual loss of prosperity for generations.

Know well the condition of your flocks,
    and give attention to your herds,
for riches do not last forever;
    and does a crown endure to all generations? (Prov 27:23-24)

Ultimate confidence in God and an enduring commitment to thoughtful wealth management are not easy to cultivate, but they are hallmarks of wise living heralded in Proverbs.

Another facet of economic diligence advocated in Proverbs is wisdom's long-term view and the prudence of delayed gratification. Investment and expenditure decisions must embrace wise priorities and take into account the timing and amount of income. "Put your outdoor work in order and get your fields ready; after that, build your house" (Prov 24:27 NIV). In our modern Western culture, immediate gratification stimulates the economy with consumer spending. However, it also fuels suffocating personal debt and encourages marginless households, who live one paycheck away from severe economic hardship. In publicly traded companies, we observe the common practice of utilizing creative accounting practices to embellish quarterly sales or profit data in order to drive stock prices up. Seeking to satisfy investors' short-term desire for a quick return, the long-term health and future profitability of companies are all too easily compromised. Economic wisdom does not ignore short-term realities, whether they appear bright or bleak, but keeps the long-term view in mind.

Economic generosity. In addition to economic integrity and economic diligence, another key component of economic wisdom that emerges in the book of Proverbs is economic generosity. It is important to grasp the symbiosis and synergy operative within this economic wisdom trinity. A virtuous person who brings value to the economic system of exchange through their diligent labor will have capacity for economic generosity. In Old Testament wisdom literature, virtue, diligence, and generosity come together as a primary means and motivation for true neighborly love. Wisdom calls for a neighborly love of compassion and capacity. Wisdom compels us forward with both compassion for the economic needs of our neighbor and the economic capacity to meet those needs through wise generosity.

In Proverbs, a primary way wisdom expresses itself is through economic generosity to the economically vulnerable and impoverished. Economic generosity not only helps the recipient and honors God, but also blesses the giver.[8] Those who are not economically generous to the poor not only miss God's blessing, they show contempt for God and their neighbor. "Whoever despises his neighbor is a sinner, but blessed is he who is generous to the poor" (Prov 14:21). "Whoever oppresses the poor shows contempt for their Maker, but whoever is kind to the needy honors God" (Prov 14:31 NIV).

Jesus' parable of the rich fool embraces themes found in Proverbs regarding economic generosity (see Lk 12:13-21). While the rich man in Jesus' story continues to acquire more and more material wealth, he closes his heart to God. Living in the black hole of self-absorption and self-indulgence, the rich fool is completely indifferent to the needs of the community. The rich fool displays contempt for God and his neighbors. His false sense of security suddenly evaporates as his life abruptly ends. The rich man's impoverished life is now on display for all to see. In the end, his unwise pursuit of wealth results in absolute ruin. Jesus' words preserved for us by the apostle Paul, reflect Proverbs' praise of economic generosity toward the economically vulnerable. Offering a proverbial sounding principle, Jesus says, "It is more blessed to give than to receive" (Acts 20:35).

A WISE PERSPECTIVE

For many years, Emmanuel Faith Community Church in Escondido, California, has emphasized discipleship initiatives and programs around marriage and family life as they seek to serve their congregation and its Southern California community. While the church continues these important areas of focus, a new whole-life discipleship emphasis is being embraced through its robust and thoughtful faith-at-work initiatives. Discipleship ministries pastor Jeremy Clark and professor Robert Harp of the Crowell School of Business at Biola University have teamed up with the enthusiastic support of the church leadership to bring transformational congregational care through stronger and more intentional faith, work, and economic integration.

A regular diet of faith at work breakfasts, seminars, and conferences is hosted by this vibrant local church congregation—not only for its congregational members but for those at other area churches who are seeking greater equipping in faith, work, and economic integration. The church is strategically using its excellent website as a resource to equip and inspire congregation members to connect Sunday worship with Monday work. Faith@Work Spotlights are popular workplace interviews and testimonies posted on the church website featuring members from a variety of workplace contexts. In these videos, individuals share their vocational journey of faith and work integration. Other resources on their website include blog posts, book reviews, journal articles, and videos of national thought leaders.

Emmanuel Faith Community shows that wisdom can be learned. It can be acquired by diligent students who apprentice themselves to thoughtful teachers. As Emmanuel's leaders have introduced the congregation to new and fresh thinking about economics, the nuance and depth of the congregation's economic perspective has grown.

Similarly, if we desire to engage economics thoughtfully and biblically, we must steep our minds in the wisdom of Proverbs, which places economic flourishing in its proper perspective. Our economic integrity, diligence, and generosity matter if we are to live well, honor God, and love our neighbor. In Proverbs we are also reminded of the goodness of economic life, but we are warned that there is much more to life than money and material wealth. We see that economics and value creation matter, but they can matter too much. Material wealth in whatever form it takes can be a wonderful servant but a cruel master. Wise economics is not only a matter of the head but also of the heart. In the end, the heart of the matter is a matter of the heart.[9]

7

WISDOM AND THE MODERN ECONOMY

Some see private enterprise as a
predatory target to be shot, others as a
cow to be milked, but few are those who see it
as a sturdy horse pulling the wagon.

WINSTON CHURCHILL

The plans of the diligent lead
surely to abundance, but everyone who
is hasty comes only to poverty.

PROVERBS 21:5

I f we are to love our neighbors wisely and to be faithful in our vocational callings, then we not only need theological insight but also sound economic thinking to guide us. In our modern economy certain foundational economic building blocks and wise economic principles promote human flourishing. Let's explore some of them.

PRIVATE PROPERTY RIGHTS

In addition to diligence of labor, a foundational building block of vibrant economies is the concept of private property rights. Property rights honored and protected by voluntary contractual agreements, insured by fair and just laws, and respected by governments who eschew corruption are foundational to human flourishing. Indeed, sound biblical theology and sound economic theory converge around the vital importance of private property rights. Theologian Robert A. Sirico wisely points out, "Societies that have a deep and unyielding respect for the sanctity of private property have traditionally fostered institutions that we associate with a vibrant social and cultural life: for example, intact families, savings and deferred gratification, cooperative social norms, and high standards of morality."[1]

Private property rights are strongly affirmed throughout Scripture. Land ownership and personal property were often seen as manifestations of God's blessing and faithfulness of divine covenant (see Gen 15:14; 30:30, 43; 33:11; 49:25-26). The sanctity of property transactions is evidenced in Abraham's purchase of the field of Machpelah from Ephron the Hittite for Sarah's burial plot (Gen 23:1-20). A detailed and integrated set of property and economic laws are articulated for the nation of Israel in the book of Leviticus (Lev 25:1-55; see also Num 27; 36). The eighth commandment prohibiting theft assumes private ownership of property (Ex 20:15).[2] Few characters in the Old Testament are portrayed as being more debased and wicked than Queen Jezebel. At the heart of Jezebel's corrupt life was her violation of personal property rights in the case of Naboth's vineyard (1 Kings 21).

Private property rights are vital to modern economies. There are many reasons for this such as risk and reward, personal incentive, future forecasting, and personal responsibility. Perhaps most important is the relationship between private property rights and capital creation. Peruvian economist Hernando de Soto, who has devoted much of his career to addressing poverty alleviation in the world, makes a compelling case that a great deal of the economic vibrancy in Western economies is due to the ensuring of private property rights and its corollary of capital acceleration. Looking through a historical lens, de Soto sees a great leap forward in economic vibrancy that coincides with the establishment of property law. He writes, "The 'something momentous' was that Americans and Europeans were on the verge of establishing widespread formal property law and inventing the conversion process in that law that allowed them to create capital."[3]

Whether we look through the illuminating lens of theology or examine the history of economic vibrancy, it is well established that personal property rights are foundational for human flourishing.[4] Yet we must not see private property rights as a license for myopic self-indulgence, but rather as legal guarantees that enable wise and generous stewardship. Our economic stewardship is a vital aspect of our life stewardship. While the Scriptures strongly affirm private property rights, the ultimate owner of all of creation is God himself. At the end of the day we stewards will be held accountable by God, stewards called to rightly love our neighbor with all that we are and have.

SELF-INTEREST

Both in Scripture and in economics, proper self-interest is a foundational building block for human flourishing. Jesus' teaching on the Great Commandment is a clarion call to proper love of self and neighbor, not a muted call to self-loathing. While emphasizing the importance of loving our neighbor rightly, Jesus makes it clear that we are to love our neighbor as we love ourselves. Self-love calls for the right stewardship of our self-interest and calls us to embrace personal responsibility to be attentive to proper self-care.

We must not emphasize neighborly love so much that we ignore proper self-love. We dare not confuse proper self-interest with sinful selfishness.[5] Human incentive based on a proper self-interest influences human behavior and motivates economic activity.[6] Steven Landsburg writes, "Most of economics can be summarized in four words: 'People respond to incentives.' The rest is commentary."[7] Proper self-interest plays an essential role in establishing the price mechanism that navigates ever-changing supply and demand, as well as in risk and reward realities within economic exchange. Economists James Gwartney, Richard Stroup, Dwight Lee, and Tawni Ferrarini observe, "The foundation of trade is mutual gain. People agree to an exchange because they expect it to improve their well-being."[8] While selfishness manifested in things like greed and exploitation can be devastating to economic vitality, proper self-interest is the fuel of incentive for economic innovation, risk taking, and expansion.

ECONOMIC OPPORTUNITY

From a biblical perspective, we were designed to cultivate blessings from the created order through our work. In and through our diligent labor, we not only meet our material needs, we also create value for others. The value we create for others is often monetized in an economic system of exchange. Throughout Scripture the opportunity to create value through our work is strongly affirmed, and when that opportunity is thwarted through unjust means it is forbidden. Old Testament laws and customs ensured that even the most marginalized and economically vulnerable were given opportunity to work and create value.[9] In that agrarian context, where land was indispensable for economic opportunity, during the Jubilee year provisions were made for return of the land to those who had needed to sell (see Lev 25). The Jubilee provision was an economic safety net of last resort to ensure economic opportunity and flourishing family life.

In modern economies the principle of providing economic opportunity is foundational to both the fairness and vitality of the social and economic ecosystem. Providing equal economic *opportunity*—not equal *outcomes*—for all is the goal that must be vigorously pursued. In our highly competitive, ever-changing, advanced technological global economy, a wide variety of outcomes will inevitably occur. There will be economic winners and losers. But this is not a bad thing. The forces of risk and reward must remain in constant tension for new ventures to be launched and new opportunities created. However, governments do have the responsibility to confront economic monopolies, because in the road of free enterprise and opportunity, monopolies are stifling roadblocks.[10] Economist Thomas Sowell makes an important clarification of what is meant by a monopoly: "The key to monopoly is not market share—even when it is 100 percent—but the ability to keep others out. A company which cannot keep competitors out is not a monopoly, no matter what percentage of the market it may have at a given moment."[11] Simply put, monopolies are enterprises that actively and effectively prevent competitors from entering the economic system. Where they indeed exist, monopolies should be resisted.

Neighborly love and sound economic thinking call us to promote policies and practices that provide economic opportunity to all—both in profit and nonprofit sectors of the economy.

MONEY AND TRADE

Throughout human history, people have traded desirable and beneficial material resources with each other. While persuasion has certainly greased many transactions, trade, by its very definition, is not coercive. Historically, the means of trade was bartering. In a barter system, one economic actor directly exchanges a particular material good with another economic actor. In biblical times, bartering was a common practice, but we also see in Scripture that various means of representative exchange were used to facilitate the transactions. Indeed, money in its many shapes and forms has allowed people to trade material goods with others for millennia. With its advent, money transformed trade, allowing the exchange of material goods to take place in a far more dynamic way. No longer did one who had an ox but wanted a goat need to find another who had a goat but wanted an ox. Instead, money could be used as a transaction tool, allowing neighbors to exchange something of value they had for something another neighbor wanted or needed. Economist Hernando de Soto notes, "After all, that is why money was invented; it provides a standing index to measure the value of things so that we can exchange dissimilar assets."[12]

In a modern economy we take money for granted. Many of us can't imagine another form of compensation or exchange. It's become second nature for us to receive a paycheck from our work, deposit it in a bank, and then use that money to buy food or clothes. A myriad of marvelous supply-and-demand decisions arbitrated by a price mechanism helps to produce, deliver, and allocate the supply and demand dynamics of an astonishing amount of services and goods. Money facilitates each value exchange transaction. Whether it takes the form of a precious metal, a paper note, or an electronic entry, in a very real way money does make the world go around.

Money and its close relationship with trade not only facilitates the transfer of goods and services, it also plays a dynamic role in creating wealth. Economist P. J. Hill creatively describes how the dynamic of wealth creation occurs through the process of trade and exchange. Hill often teaches this important economic truth by what is known as "the trading game." In the trading game every participant is given a bag containing an item and two cards. To start, each participant writes on a card the value they'd assign to the item in their bag. Then those cards are collected. Next, participants are encouraged to actively trade their items with others. For several minutes, students swap the items they received, making trade after trade. At the end of the trading time, each participant is asked to assign a value to the item they came to possess and write it on the remaining card. In the trading game the value on the second card is always larger than the first because each student performed trades they believed to be in their best interest. On a microscale, the trading game demonstrates how trade and exchange actually create new wealth.[13] It is not hard then to imagine how wealth expands on a macroscale within a multitrillion-dollar global economy.

The close relationship between trade and money in modern economies speaks to the importance of wise government fiscal policy and currency stability. Rampant inflation, spiraling deflation, or wild swings in currency valuations are highly disruptive, wreaking havoc in any economic system of exchange. Economic uncertainty and unpredictability raise the level of perceived risk and thereby cripple innovation, capital investment, and consumer confidence.

Often, money is seen as intrinsically bad or perhaps a necessary evil in the world, but we must not forget the important role money plays in wealth creation and in facilitating the efficient exchange of goods and services. Money, and the trade it makes possible, furthers the common good and greatly enhances our ability to love our neighbors—both local and global. Dallas Willard rightly reminds us, "Business is an amazingly effective means of delivering God's love to the world by loving, serving and providing for one another."[14] While it is true that business and commerce often fall short of meeting the neighborly love standard and do not always promote an economics of mutuality, the importance of for-profit enterprises must not be discredited.

The idea of profit can at first blush seem problematic, but on closer reflection we can see the importance of profit within an economic system. When property rights are well defined and contracts are consistently enforced, profits perform an important function within modern economies. Profits provide rewards for technological innovation and resource efficiency in delivering goods and services to others. In this sense, profits are important incentives for promoting research and development, enabling enterprises to discover superior products and better ways to meet the needs of people.

Within a modern economy, profits are also a signaling mechanism encouraging others to devote more resources in that particular market opportunity. I remember fishing on one of Minnesota's ten thousand lakes as a young boy. When the fish started biting in one particular part of the lake, it didn't take long for a crowd of boats to show up and take advantage of the promising opportunity. Like fish that are biting, profits also draw crowds. Profits can and do at times bring out the worst in economic actors, but in many ways profit mechanisms encourage people to look out for others and to serve them in better ways. On a practical side, profits also are vital to government and nonprofit organizations because these important sectors of society depend on the economic engine of for-profit enterprises for their success.

The apostle Paul, who like Jesus spoke a great deal about money, makes it clear that it is not money per se but rather an inordinate love of money that must be avoided. Writing to Timothy, Paul states, "For the love of money is a root of all kinds of evils. It is through this craving that some have wandered away from the faith and pierced themselves with many pangs" (1 Tim 6:10). Economic wisdom pushes back at the idolatrous idea that money is the ultimate good. Indeed, much of the value created in the world is never monetized. Money is never to be worshiped. Only God deserves that. But money is a remarkably helpful servant, and the good that it generates and facilitates should be recognized.

Bishop Larry Ward, the pastor of Abundant Life Church in Cambridge, Massachusetts, has been at the forefront of the integration of faith, work, and economics. He has sought to help his congregation understand the importance of entrepreneurship and profit within an economic system. Partnering with David Gill at Gordon-Conwell Theological Seminary, Larry has taught courses to seminary students on economics and business. He and his staff have also creatively integrated a robust theology of faith, work, and economics into their church youth education efforts. In place of a traditional Vacation Bible School, Abundant Life sponsors a BIZ Camp, which focuses on how the gospel speaks into entrepreneurship. At the BIZ camp, youth are taught how to develop business plans. Seasoned business leaders who bring business savvy as well as intergenerational modeling are recruited to serve as sounding boards to help these aspiring teenagers fine-tune their business plans and eventually launch new businesses.

While in high school, Bishop Ward's son noticed students were unable to purchase snacks from the school's vending machines because they were too expensive. So his son bought an inventory of snacks and sold them below the prices of the vending machines but at prices that allowed him to make a profit. His small business was wildly successful. Ultimately, the vendors removed their machines due to lack of sales. It is exciting to think that these bright students in BIZ Camps today will soon be launching real-world organizations for the good of their communities.

SPECIALIZATION

Both Christian anthropology and our daily life experience tell us humans have differing ability and skills. Most likely, my dentist would be a poor professional dancer. I doubt whether a cardiologist friend would perform very well on a professional football team. I, a pastor, would make a pitiful auto mechanic. When the work we do fits well with our capabilities, we not only benefit from the satisfaction of good work well done, our neighbors benefit from our strong value creation. Specialization of labor makes sense as a foundational building block in modern economies. Specialization also reflects God's design.

From the opening pages of Holy Scripture we observe a variety of work done by a variety of people. In Genesis we observe a division of labor between Abel and Cain. Abel becomes a shepherd and Cain a farmer. Bezalel and Oholiab were highly skilled craftsmen in the building trades. Both were given supernatural empowerment by the Holy Spirit to do their work. While Bezalel and Oholiab are singled out because of their special skills, it is important that we don't neglect God's assertion to Moses that all people have been given ability for the work they are to do in the world (Ex 31:6).

In the New Testament we read that a variety of spiritual gifts have been given to the church by the Holy Spirit. The repeated depiction of the church as a body reminds us that interdependent specialization is required for the vitality and flourishing of the whole community (see 1 Cor 12). A flourishing local church is a compelling picture of the goodness of interdependent specialization within an economy. We must also remember common-grace talents and spiritual gifts operate not only within the church on Sunday but also within the workplace on Monday. We not only walk in the Spirit, we work in the Spirit.

Doing work that suits our genetic wiring and developed skills within an economic system that rewards and utilizes specialization catapults economic efficiency and productivity. With specialization, costs of production fall and economies of scale emerge. Higher quantities and better quality products and services are produced. Undergirding specialization are well-enforced property rights. In a modern economy the price mechanism also plays a crucial role in specialization. Leonard Read's literary essay "I Pencil" captures the remarkable web of specialization and collaboration. Read's description of the millions of people involved in the production, advertising, transportation, and sale of one lead pencil is truly eye opening.[15]

On the whole, greater specialization of human work, as well as the technology that makes it possible, has greatly contributed to increased human flourishing. Economist's Victor Claar and Robin Klay point to specialization as a crucial component for raising the standard of living in much of the world today. "As a result of extensive labor specialization in larger and more capital intensive markets, the vast majority of people living today in advanced economies like the United States, the European Union, Australia, and Japan enjoy a material standard of living far superior to that of even kings of old."[16]

It is also true that greater division of labor and work specialization have brought unintended consequences, at times dehumanizing work, and extracting meaning from human labor. The worker on an assembly line who inserts rivets into a metal panel all day might find that task mundane and toilsome. With greater work specialization, it is often difficult to find meaning in work or to take pride in the collective contribution being made by the process, because workers are separated from the final product that is created and the good value it creates for the customer. With greater specialization comes a greater need for managers to intentionally present a comprehensive picture of the goals and mission motivating the organization. Those who start and operate business enterprises also have a responsibility to nurture workplaces that enhance flourishing for all and that seek to keep specialization from robbing people of dignity and meaning in their work.

LEGAL SYSTEMS AND INSTITUTIONS

Although the scope of government involvement in economics is debated, there is consensus that government has a role to play in a vibrant economy. Governments in a modern economy are actively involved in a host of ways.[17] In a broken world filled with broken people, economic actors need rules and boundaries for economic exchange. Fair and just laws enforced consistently are crucial. The apostle Paul makes the case that government is to serve as a minister of God, promoting the common good, protecting citizens, and confronting wrongdoing (Rom 13:1-5). Paul also affirms the legitimacy of government within an economic system, particularly in regard to taxation (Rom 13:6-7). Like all human institutions, government can lose its way in the suffocating weeds of bureaucratic expansion, regulation overreach, outright coercion, and monetary corruption. In voting democracies with representative government, the governed have a nonviolent means in which to bring change to government when it is needed.

Financial institutions also play a vital role in facilitating well-functioning capital markets. Institutions like banks serve as intermediaries in economic exchange. Banks also facilitate borrowing and saving, and provide a stable and secure means for financial liquidity. Bond markets bring borrowers and investors together in a mutually benefiting relationship. Stock markets make it possible for corporations to raise capital and for investors to gain partial ownership with the hope of sharing in future profits. Financial institutions like insurance companies help manage economic risk. Within the vast financial service industry, a wide variety of financial products have been created that make possible a wide diversification of investments to both individual and institutional investors.

The institution of the family also plays a vital role in economic flourishing. In many ways the family is the most basic economic unit in the economy. We've already seen that our English word *economics* comes from a Greek word *oikonomia*, which connotes the idea of household or family stewardship. There is a seamless, interdependent relationship between family life, the workplace, and the broader economy. In a real sense, as the family unit flourishes, the broader economy flourishes. The family's procreativity provides the labor force for the economy. Much of the intellectual and social capital the economy depends on finds its source in the dynamic and nourishing womb of family life. Whether or not family members are virtuous, innovative, and productive affects the economy. In the context of the family many economic decisions are made, and children are taught the basics of microeconomics and learn the realities of macroeconomic life. In addition to the family, educational institutions such as colleges and universities provide ongoing instruction in economics while taking on new lines of research. The institutions of government, finance, family, and education all play an indispensable role in a flourishing modern economy.

HOPEFUL REALISM

A firmer grasp of theology and a better understanding of economic history ought to guard us against any form of visionary utopian dreaming. It also should prevent us from blind ideological economic conformity, passivity, or indifference. The economy matters. The economy matters to God. The economy matters to our neighbor. The economy ought to matter to us. While we are broken people living in broken communities, we have a sovereign God who has revealed to us economic wisdom both in the common grace of general revelation as well as through the saving grace of biblical revelation.

When we learn and apply economic wisdom, we can be hopeful that economic injustice can be confronted, economic opportunity can be offered, and economic flourishing can be a reality, even for the most vulnerable and marginalized of society. While some economic theories and frameworks are better than others in producing human flourishing, they all can be distorted and corrupted. Economic progress can be achieved, yet economic perfection will only come when Jesus returns and establishes his perfect reign in the new heavens and new earth. In this already–not yet moment of redemptive history, economic wisdom that comes from Scripture as well as sound economic understanding articulated by thoughtful economists will move us in the direction of a God-honoring humble confidence, hopeful realism, and greater human flourishing.

Many leaders and entrepreneurs have embraced economic wisdom for the good of others, adding value to the world. One of those leaders is Paige Chenault, who has launched and led thriving organizations in both the for-profit and nonprofit sectors. In 2005 Paige launched an event-planning company. By 2011 that company was handling over $4 million dollars in projects each year. In 2012 Paige founded the Birthday Party Project, a nonprofit organization that partners with local agencies to host birthday parties for homeless children across the country. Paige has an entrepreneur's mind and a gospel-saturated heart, and both work together seamlessly as she creates environments of joy and flourishing using her business acumen and organizational leadership skills. Paige is an example of how gospel compassion should put on economic hands and feet. Stories like Paige's should encourage and inspire us to pursue economic wisdom so that we might bless our neighbors.[18]

A VERY WISE WOMAN

While the book of Proverbs opens with a focus on King Solomon, it closes by showcasing a wise woman. It is not incidental that the pinnacle of proverbial wisdom is not personified by a king or a priest, but rather by a fruitful woman whose wisdom-laden life exhibits the fruit of procreativity and productivity. She is a woman who indwells her creation design and is faithful to fulfill her creation mandate as a fruitful image-bearer of God. The highly esteemed woman presented in Proverbs 31 stands as the crescendo of wisdom's economic vision. Here we see individuals and society encouraged to produce wealth and income within an economic system that affirms diligent labor and the goodness of profit. Economic integrity, diligence, and generosity are all on display in the decisions and disposition of this virtuous woman, who stewards her economic capacity for the love of God, family, and neighbor.

> She seeks wool and flax,
>   and works with willing hands.
> She is like the ships of the merchant;
>   she brings her food from afar.
> She rises while it is yet night
>   and provides food for her household
>   and portions for her maidens.
> She considers a field and buys it;
>   with the fruit of her hands she plants a vineyard.
> She dresses herself with strength
>   and makes her arms strong.
> She perceives that her merchandise is profitable.
>   Her lamp does not go out at night.
> She puts her hands to the distaff,
>   and her hands hold the spindle.
> She opens her hand to the poor
>   and reaches out her hands to the needy.
> She is not afraid of snow for her household,
>   for all her household are clothed in scarlet.
> She makes bed coverings for herself;
>   her clothing is fine linen and purple.

Her husband is known in the gates
    when he sits among the elders of the land.
She makes linen garments and sells them;
    she delivers sashes to the merchant.
Strength and dignity are her clothing,
    and she laughs at the time to come.
She opens her mouth with wisdom,
    and the teaching of kindness is on her tongue.
She looks well to the ways of her household
    and does not eat the bread of idleness.
Her children rise up and call her blessed;
    her husband also, and he praises her:
"Many women have done excellently,
    but you surpass them all."
Charm is deceitful, and beauty is vain,
    but a woman who fears the LORD is to be praised.
Give her of the fruit of her hands,
    and let her works praise her in the gates. (Prov 31:13-31)

8

WISE GENEROSITY

*How do modern Christians and churches
avoid the seductive power of material possessions?
How can wealth remain a "good" for their enjoyment rather
than leading them further away from God and the priorities
of his kingdom? The recurring answer of both Testaments
is through generous giving to others.*

CRAIG BLOMBERG

*Honor the LORD with your wealth
and with the firstfruits of all your produce;
then your barns will be filled with plenty,
and your vats will be bursting with wine.*

PROVERBS 3:9-10

Hardly a day goes by when we are not presented with an opportunity for financial generosity. Whether we meet a homeless person on the street, receive an emotional appeal to help feed malnourished children in our inbox, learn of an opportunity to meet prenatal care needs in Haiti, open an invitation to attend a fundraiser for a local parachurch organization, or contemplate a pledge to our local church's capital funding initiative, opportunities for generosity abound. Facing this myriad of giving opportunities brought to us by a host of sophisticated fundraising strategies from experts in the nonprofit sector, we are confronted with a complex challenge. We are called to love our neighbors with a generous love characterized by Christian compassion and economic capacity, but how should we wisely navigate the challenging terrain of local and global philanthropy?

A GENEROSITY REVOLUTION

When it comes to generosity in our contemporary culture there is some good news and some not so good news. First, the good news: We live in a time when a greater awareness and emphasis is being placed on generosity. Billionaires Bill and Melinda Gates along with Warren Buffet have led the way in encouraging the world's wealthiest to sign the Giving Pledge, a public commitment designed to hold its signatories accountable to donating the majority of their wealth to efforts and initiatives focused on increasing human flourishing.[1] This is remarkably encouraging.

Even as the widening wealth gap is a growing concern for many—with $7.7 trillion being controlled by the world's billionaires—it is important to recognize that though the number of billionaires is growing, billionaires only control 3.9 percent of the world's wealth.[2] While we ought to be grateful for a growing sense of responsibility among the wealthiest of the world to promote the common good, we must also own the truth that each of us need to take seriously our own responsibility to be generous, no matter our financial position.

Echoes of a generosity revolution are also being heard with increasing frequency and passion in many Christian faith communities.[3] Of course, this is good news and must be applauded by thoughtful followers of Jesus. Every one of us is called to be generous with our financial resources. After all, Jesus said, "It is more blessed to give than to receive" (Acts 20:35). The not-so-good news is that while we are hearing more calls to live generously, less emphasis is being placed on how we are to be generous.

It is increasingly common for me to be approached by individuals wrestling with decisions regarding their financial giving. I'm often asked, "What principles ought to guide me in making a wise generosity decision?" "Where should I give to and why?" "Should I give now or invest with the intent of hopefully having more to give later?" "What about giving to individuals versus to institutions?"

Thoughtful followers of Jesus wrestle with where to give their financial resources because wise stewardship is important. Biblical generosity is not just about giving a particular amount or giving with a particular attitude, but also about giving according to particular wisdom. Generosity without wisdom is a very real challenge we all face. Our generous giving must not only flow from a generous heart but also be guided by a thoughtful mind.

In the city where I live there is an annual celebration of generosity. A large banquet highlights the good work that several Christian organizations do in our community. Each award recipient walks the red carpet to well-deserved applause and receives a sizeable check to further their not-for-profit endeavors. While I affirm the goodness of celebrating generosity, I often feel a tug of war in my heart. On the one hand, I am thrilled by the refreshing demonstration of generosity, but on the other, I inevitably feel some inescapable dissonance. Was this demonstration of generosity directed in such a way that it would be deemed as wise stewardship? Did the generosity celebrated have a short-term or a long-term view in mind? Why were local churches not featured or considered for awards? Why have local churches been virtually absent at the celebration of generosity in our city? What would Jesus think about this banquet?

Jesus cared not only about generosity but also about wise financial stewardship. In one of Jesus' most sobering parables, three individuals were entrusted with varying degrees of financial resources and only two of them were deemed wise stewards and received the coveted accolade of "good and faithful servant" (Mt 25:14-30).

WISELY STEWARDED GENEROSITY

Each one of us must reflectively and prayerfully ask, Is my generosity being stewarded wisely?[4] We must not only grow in generosity, we must also grow in the wise stewardship of our generosity. In our quest for greater generosity, are we missing the mark of wise stewardship? Are we investing God's financial resources wisely? What considerations ought to guide us in pursuing wise stewardship? As we discover *that* God designed us to be generous, are we also discovering *how* God has designed us to be generous?

If we begin to more firmly grasp God's design on how we should direct our generosity, the revolution of generosity we are graciously experiencing in our time will have profound and lasting impact for the gospel and the common good. But if we are unwise with how our generosity is directed, we will miss the wide-open door of opportunity before us in this strategic moment in redemptive history.

DESIGN-BASED GIVING

If we are going to be wise stewards, and if we are going to foster a God-honoring culture of wise generosity, we will need to embrace a giving approach based on God's design. This giving approach is what I like to refer to as "design-based giving." Design-based giving challenges us to reconsider our generosity paradigm, reorder our heart loves, and reprioritize our giving. Before we press further into a design-based giving approach, perhaps a bit more definition of what I mean by this term would be helpful.

As followers of Christ, we believe God has a design for how we are to live. We believe this design is revealed to us in Scripture. Made in the image of a generous, outpouring God, we were designed to be generous with our time, talents, and treasures. Design-based giving not only recognizes we are to be generous but also understands that God has given us a design template for how we are to give. At the heart of this design is a gracious generosity that looks through the lens of Scripture and sees the local church as the primary focus of our financial giving.

Scripture presents to us a design for true human flourishing and the collective common good. As image bearers of the triune God, we were created to be generous by one whose very nature is generous outpouring.[5] Harold Best insightfully makes the point, "Because God is the Continuous Outpourer, we bear his image as continuous outpourers. Being made in the image of God means that we were created to act as God acts, having been given a nature within which such behavior is natural."[6] Each one of us has been created by a generous God to be generous. We were created not with a closed fist but with open hands. An unwillingness to be generous or a decision to embrace a selfish greed goes against the grain of our original creation nature and design. In this sense, nothing is more unnatural than a person lacking generosity. Jesus' words "it is more blessed to give than to receive" affirm this bedrock theological truth anchored in Creation design.

Though sin entered God's good world, marring the divine image we were created to reflect, our generous God sent his Son Jesus to this sin-scarred earth to shed his atoning blood on a cruel Roman cross. The apostle Paul describes the generous outpouring of our salvation:

When the goodness and loving kindness of God our Savior appeared, he saved us, not because of works done by us in righteousness, but according to his own mercy, by the washing of regeneration and renewal of the Holy Spirit, whom he poured out on us richly through Jesus Christ our Savior. (Titus 3:4-6)

When we in faith and repentance embrace the gospel, we are not only forgiven of our sin, we become new creations in Christ. As new-creation individuals originally created to be generous, we are recreated to be generous. We are called into a new-creation community, the local church, where generosity finds its full and collective expression. Though it is beyond my scope to highlight the many biblical texts that speak of being generous and good stewards of our financial treasure, I would like to erect a theologically informed, paradigmatic scaffolding for giving based upon three bedrock ideas: (1) God owns it all; (2) we give God our best; and (3) the local church is plan A for the world.

God owns it all. At its very heart, design-based giving embraces the bedrock truth that as Creator, God owns it all. The psalmist declares that "the earth is the LORD's, and everything in it" (Ps 24:1 NIV). The writer of Chronicles echoes this foundational truth: "Yours, O LORD, is the greatness and the power and the glory and the victory and the majesty, for all that is in the heavens and in the earth is yours. Yours is the kingdom, O LORD, and you are exalted as head above all. Both riches and honor come from you, and you rule over all" (1 Chron 29:11-12). Because God owns it all, we recognize that all our financial assets belong to him.

We are stewards of the time, talent, and treasure entrusted to us as Jesus' yoked apprentices. Randy Alcorn rightly places stewardship in its foundational place within the Christian faith.

Stewardship is not a subcategory of the Christian life. Stewardship is the Christian life. For what is stewardship but that God has entrusted to us life, time, talents, money, possessions, family, his grace and even his Son? In each case he evaluates how we regard and what we do with that which he has entrusted to us. . . .

It is living life with the acute awareness that we are managers, not owners, that we are caretakers of God's assets, which he has entrusted to us while we are on earth. How we handle our money and possessions will be determined by whom we really believe to be their true owner—and ours.[7]

We are stewards who will be held accountable for what we have done with what we have been given. The sobering reality is this: We are not owners but managers. This truth must stay in front of us and remind us that our wealth and economic capacity are not ours to do with as we please. Rather, we must do with them what the true Owner would desire.

Giving God our best. Design-based giving not only embraces the bedrock truth that God owns it all, it also affirms that we are called to give our very best. The writer of Proverbs reminds us that we honor God by giving God the first fruits of both our income and wealth. The first fruits of our economic activity and productivity are to be an offering to God.[8] In other words, the first check we write each pay period and the first consideration in our yearly financial plan, as well as in our long-term estate planning, should be focused on our God-honoring generosity.

Making financial giving our highest budgetary priority is most often not a matter of the head but of the heart. Jesus reminds us that if we get our economic treasure right, our heart will follow.[9] Perhaps no place in the New Testament is this truth more vividly expressed than in Jesus' encounter with Zacchaeus, a chief tax collector.

Embracing Jesus as his Messiah, Zacchaeus immediately realizes the implication for his wealth. He says to Jesus, "Behold, Lord, the half of my goods I give to the poor. And if I have defrauded anyone of anything, I restore it fourfold" (Lk 19:8). When Jesus sees that Zacchaeus is putting his treasure in the right place, he knows his heart is in the right place. John Schneider looks to the transformation of Zacchaeus: "In this story it is not that a man is saved from the economics of the world, but that the world is redeemed in and through the salvation and the new economics of the man."[10] The primacy of giving God our best both in proper motive and substance is also seen in the contrast in giving between Barnabas and Ananias and Sapphira. While Barnabas gives his very best, Ananias and Sapphira deceptively create the illusion they have given their best when they have not. The severity of the consequences resulting from their stewardship deception should make us shudder (see Acts 5:1-11).

When we give God our best, we start with the foundational baseline of tithing. Throughout the Old Testament, God's covenant people offered God their tithes and offerings in the context and place of their corporate worship. For example, the renewal of God's covenant people in the time of Nehemiah emphasized the generous giving of God's people as it was directed toward the house of God (see Neh 10). Sometimes, when we read the design for giving presented in the Old Testament, we push back against it, saying it is a form of legalism. In those private conversations of the soul, we persuade ourselves that things are vastly different in the New Testament. But if we take a closer look at the Scriptures, we see a great deal of continuity between the Old and the New Testaments.[11] Not only does the apostle Paul use the language of the "household of God" to describe the local church (1 Tim 3:15), the witness and history of the early church points toward regular giving that occurred above and beyond the baseline of tithing (see Acts 2:44-45; 4:34-35). We also observe in the New Testament that the local church is the primary recipient of the Christ-follower's generous giving.

The local church as plan A. Design-based giving embraces the bedrock truth that the local church is "plan A" for God's purposes in the world. In Scripture, institutions matter. The institution of marriage and the church as an institution are central to God's creation mandate and redemptive mission. Just as God created the institution of marriage to carry forward his redemptive plan, he likewise created the local church as the central path through which humankind is to exercise dominion and fulfill God's kingdom purposes in the world. God did not design his redeemed world to be filled with isolated, redeemed individuals. Rather, he desires new creation communities, bound together in common purpose, to flourish in particular places and times.[12]

When we speak of institutions and the institutional nature of the local church, we affirm the necessity and wisdom of ongoing organizational structures that make possible a long-established, faithful church presence in a particular geographic setting. When the New Testament speaks of the church, its primary focus is the local church.[13] The apostles interpreted Jesus' words that he would build his church as a clear and compelling mandate for planting local churches throughout the world. The planting and multiplication of local churches throughout the book of Acts demonstrates that the apostles understood the local church to be uniquely designed and gifted by the Spirit to be God's plan A for fulfilling both the Great Commandment and the Great Commission.

The local church, as Christ designed it and indwells it, is both a growing organism as well as an ongoing institution. Throughout the book of Acts we not only see the transformation of individuals as the gospel is proclaimed, we also see the intentional establishment of local church structures with institutional organization that supports this organic growth. Local churches were planted, and embryonic leadership structures were quickly established that allowed these churches to eventually become more fully developed institutions, with increased numerical size and sociological complexity. Because of this institutional design, local churches are able to establish an ongoing faithful presence in a community that transcends any one individual.[14] This faithful presence allows for the continued fulfillment of the church's mandate to be salt and light in a particular cultural context, contributing to the common good and presenting an ongoing, incarnational apologetic for the gospel.

FOGGY THINKING ABOUT "GRACE GIVING"

While there is strong biblical support for design-based giving, there remains a good deal of foggy thinking around God-honoring generosity, particularly concerning what is often described as "grace giving." One reason for this all-too-prevalent distortion is a misunderstanding of Paul's teaching on matters of giving. While writing to the local church at Corinth, Paul says, "Each of you should give what you have decided in your heart to give; not reluctantly or under compulsion, for God loves a cheerful giver" (2 Cor 9:7 NIV). Is Paul saying our economic giving is to be guided solely by what feels right? Is individual subjective sentiment to be the guiding light when it comes to my giving decisions? I don't believe so.

Paul's inspired words must be seen in their proper context. Paul's letter to the local church in Corinth was written as he was traveling on his way back to Jerusalem. Along with a group of his companions, he was taking a special one-time collection from the local churches he had planted throughout Asia Minor. This collection was going to support the local church in Jerusalem, which was facing financial difficulty. Yet in spite of the clear context of Paul's financial appeal, this text is commonly used to promote the idea that we are free to give to whatever or whomever we desire.

That is simply not the case. Grace is an integral aspect of our Christian faith, but it can also be adulterated into unbiblical cheap grace of religious apathy and unfettered license. Randy Alcorn helps us see through the mirage of "grace giving": "To most people the term 'grace giving' simply means 'give what you feel like.' The problem is most Christians just don't feel like giving. And many of them never will because they are not being taught to give. As the Law was a tutor to lead us to Christ, so the tithe is a tutor that leads us on to giving."[15]

A careful reading of 2 Corinthians reveals that Paul is not speaking to the Corinthians about their baseline obedience to tithe or give first fruits. Rather, he is speaking of giving above and beyond the Corinthian believers' regular financial support of their local church. Paul is not exhorting those in the Corinthian church to give whatever they feel like. Rather, Paul is saying that when it comes to above-and-beyond sacrificial giving, individuals retain the freedom to decide if or how much to give as a matter of conscience. In truth, Paul is prodding the Corinthians toward a greater lifestyle of generosity.

In the early church, above-and-beyond giving was not to be dictated by anyone, but to be done voluntarily from the heart according to the Spirit's leading. The early church's redistribution of wealth and the giving of Barnabas, for example, reflect this kind of voluntary, above-and-beyond "grace giving" (Acts 2:42-47; 4:32-37). It is also important to observe that expressions of above-and-beyond giving were not given individual to individual but to and through the local church the giver belonged to.

When Paul's inspired words to the believers in the local church at Corinth are taken out of context and presented as the guiding template for giving in the New Testament, we perpetuate a biblical distortion and reinforce a broader cultural context that is highly individualistic, pragmatic, and anti-institutional. Because we breathe this cultural air and swim each day in the fast-moving currents of individualism, pragmatism, and anti-institutionalism, our generosity paradigms can easily become distorted. In many cases we are blind to the unintended consequences of this reality. All too often the confusion between first-fruits giving and grace giving leads to creative rationalizations for not tithing to a local church.

I have heard many rationalizations for not faithfully supporting the local church, such as "my tithe goes to a missionary," "I give my tithe to parachurch organizations," "I am helping a family member get through college," or "I have a neighbor who is in need." The capacity for rationalization is endless. Like the good Samaritan, we are to be available and generous in helping someone in immediate need. This is the calling of every true follower of Jesus, but it doesn't relieve us of the privilege and responsibility to generously support our local church. Giving to a worthy parachurch organization is a good thing, but this is not a substitute for local-church giving. Giving in addition to our local church responsibility calls each of us to cultivate greater economic capacity and to embrace nonindulgent lifestyles where increased economic generosity is made possible. We are not to negate our responsibility for honoring God's design by tithing to the household of God, our local church. In the Old Testament the failure to do this was rightly labeled "robbing" God (Mal 3:8). It is hard to imagine that somehow the definition of robbing God changes in the New Testament. Robbery is robbery no matter how you look at it.

Properly understood, the biblical framework of design-based giving assists us in making wise stewardship decisions regarding the directional outflow of our generous giving. When we embrace design-based giving, we understand that God owns it all, that tithing to the local church is the baseline of God-honoring obedience, and that the local church is God's plan A for his redemptive purposes. The local church as both an organism and an institution is designed to be an ongoing faithful presence in a community, and is irreplaceable in its effectiveness for gospel proclamation and gospel mission in the world.

SEEING THE LOCAL CHURCH DIFFERENTLY

I remember a conversation with a generous individual about embracing a design-based giving approach. He looked at me and said, "If I gave a large financial gift to my local church, they wouldn't know what to do with it." This is a common concern, but what is driving it? When we interacted more, it became obvious that what concerned this individual most was not so much what a local church might do with this amount of money, but rather what he imagined the local church to be. The same is true for many generous people today. We must begin to grasp both the amazing importance and the stunning breadth of the local church and its mission in the world. The local church, as God designed it, is the primary means through which Jesus' prayer "Your kingdom come, your will be done, on earth as it is in heaven" (Mt 6:10) is ultimately answered.[16]

As apprentices of Jesus, our own spiritual growth is tied to our immersive life within a local church community. We need the local church and the local church needs us. Philip Yancey speaks transparently yet insightfully about his own up and down pilgrimage with the local church: "Christianity is not a purely intellectual, internal faith. It can only be lived in community. Perhaps for this reason, I have never entirely given up on church. At a deep level I sense that church contains something I desperately need."[17] Our spiritual growth involves the transformation of our minds, which leads us to think differently about all of life, including the church and the ways it is inextricably linked to Christ-honoring generosity and wise financial stewardship. In writing to the local church at Rome, Paul highlights the renewal of our minds and calls for a proper response of a worshipful life of submission and obedience to Christ.

> I appeal to you therefore, brothers, by the mercies of God, to present your bodies as a living sacrifice, holy and acceptable to God, which is your spiritual worship. Do not be conformed to this world, but be transformed by the renewal of your mind, that by testing you may discern what is the will of God, what is good and acceptable and perfect. (Rom 12:1-2)

If we are going to discern and do God's will when it comes to wise generosity, we need to think differently about the local church.

The work and mission of the local church is multifaceted, but one of its stewardships is the spiritual formation of a generous congregation. A vital part of spiritual formation is growing in economic understanding, financial management, work productivity, and generosity. In this sense the local church is a school of generosity. Along with the family, the local church is a primary teacher of economic well-being and human flourishing. The macroeconomic flourishing of a community or a city is often tied to the microeconomic flourishing of individual households and family financial health. Nurturing economic capacity and wise money management is a vital aspect of local church discipleship. R. Scott Rodin says it well: "The church should be the center for developing Christians' understanding of generosity and nurturing their heart transformation."[18] Pastor Ben Patterson gets to the heart of the matter: "There is no such thing as being right with God and wrong with money."[19]

REORDERING OUR HEART LOVES

Design-based giving not only requires a renewing of the mind, it also requires a change of heart. Biblical discipleship inevitably leads us to reorder our heart loves. One of the places where this occurs is in Jesus' restoration of Peter, described for us in John's Gospel.

Peter had blown it big time. He had done the unthinkable in deserting and denying his Master, who had been crucified. But then he'd seen the empty tomb and met the living Christ. Even as the reality of Jesus' resurrection sets in, Peter remains disillusioned over the remarkable events that he had experienced. He tells his friends he's going fishing. After an entire night of catching nothing, Peter returns to the shoreline, where Jesus is waiting, making breakfast. Pulling Peter aside, Jesus asks Peter three times, "Do you love me?" And three times, Jesus tells Peter, "Take care of my sheep." In restoring a very discouraged and disillusioned Peter, Jesus' primary focus is not on what Peter believes but on what Peter loves. Our Lord's response to Peter about taking care of his sheep shows that Jesus is not only interested in Peter loving Jesus himself—as important as that is—but also in Peter loving what Jesus loves.

What does Jesus love? We could answer this question in a myriad of ways. I remember singing as a kid in Sunday school, "Jesus loves the little children, all the children of the world." Certainly, the lyrics of this song find strong support in Scripture. However, we could also strongly affirm that God not only loves the children of the world but also the totality of his good creation, for he repeatedly declared it good. Our heavenly Father extends his common grace to his world, even though it is presently marred by sin. Jesus loves the poor, the vulnerable, and the marginalized of society. Yet in Jesus' restoration of Peter we see the affectionate heart of our Lord for his redeemed people, his called out ones, the church.

As Jesus restores Peter, not only does Peter gain soul-transforming forgiveness, he also gains greater appreciation for how much Jesus cherishes his redeemed people. We know Jesus' tender words got through to Peter's mind and heart, for the aging apostle later used imagery of shepherds and flocks to speak of the affectionate stewardship of local church leadership. For the apostle Peter, loving what Jesus loved meant first and foremost taking care of Christ's sheep. Like King David, Peter grasped that redeemed people were unimaginably precious as God's own inheritance. Sometimes we hear explicitly or implicitly that people love Jesus but don't like the local church. Loving Jesus and not loving the local church would have been inconceivable for Peter. It is also inconceivable to Jesus.

LOVING JESUS' BRIDE

Though Scripture employs many metaphors to describe the beautiful design and importance of the church, the metaphor of a bride gives us a picture of how much Jesus cherishes the church. In Ephesians Paul emphasizes the reordering of our heart loves toward Christ's bride, the church. Indeed, human marriage is presented as a reflection of Christ's relationship to the church. Because Christ loves his bride, we are to cherish the church (Eph 5:25-32). The primary thrust of Paul's teaching in Ephesians is directed toward local church life. Here we see the amazing interweaving of God's complementary design for the two primary institutions he has established for his glory and the accomplishment of his redemptive purposes: the family and the local church.

Just as our Lord Jesus gently confronted Peter's improperly ordered loves, I believe he also wants to lovingly and gently confront us regarding what and how we love. Jesus calls us to love what he so deeply loves. As apprentices, we learn not only how to live like Jesus would if he were us, but over time and in the transforming power of the Holy Spirit we become increasingly like him. As we become more like Jesus we share the affections of his heart. In his easy yoke, our affections progressively change, and the primary focus of our heart becomes Jesus himself and the local expression of his church, which we are providentially called to love and serve.

Jesus loves you and me, and he loves us, his bride. Jesus shed his blood for his bride. Why wouldn't we cherish, nourish, care for, and protect the local expression of the bride he has called us to? If we truly love Jesus, we will love his bride, the church. And if we are willing to be transparent, all too often we lack a growing affectionate love for the local church.

One aspect of loving Christ's bride—a vital one—is our generous first-fruit giving, as well as Spirit-led, conscience-informed above-and-beyond giving. Design-based giving requires loving what Jesus loves, and reflects a properly ordered heart.[20] Randy Alcorn reflects a right understanding of the local church and the importance of rightly ordered loves: "Do you want your heart to be in your church? Give money to your church. Your heart will never be where your money isn't. It will be where your money is."[21] If embraced wholeheartedly, design-based giving provides a local church with the economic resources necessary to empower its catalytic gospel mission for the good of others, to the glory of Christ.

9

THE POOR AMONG US

[A] rock-star preaches capitalism. Wow.
Sometimes I hear myself and I just can't believe it.
But commerce is real. . . . Aid is just a stopgap.
Commerce—entrepreneurial capitalism—takes
more people out of poverty than aid.

BONO, GEORGETOWN UNIVERSITY SPEECH

By this we know love, that he laid down his life for us, and we
ought to lay down our lives for the brothers. But if anyone has
the world's goods and sees his brother in need, yet closes his
heart against him, how does God's love abide in him?

1 JOHN 3:16-17

The frayed and faded cardboard sign reads, "Hungry and homeless please help." I see it often as I pull up to a busy intersection on my way to work. Holding the sign—rain, snow, or shine—is an unshaven, middle-aged man wearing tattered, dirty clothes. He displays it for all to see, identifying himself as a materially impoverished beggar.

Thousands of cars pass by him each morning. Only a rare few stop. Now and then, a dollar is placed in his hands. Our eyes have met on more than one occasion when the red light refuses to turn green. The raised window thinly separates our vastly different worlds. There is an awkwardness that fills the air between us. I don't know his name, nor do I know his story. I doubt if any of my fellow drivers do either, yet he is a part of the suburban landscape I inhabit much like Starbucks, Chipotle, or McDonald's.

Each time I pass him, I am reminded that not all my fellow image bearers live as I live. I often take for granted the rich blessings of a safe and comfortable home, a nutritious diet, a job I love, and the sense of belonging I feel in a close-knit community of family and friends. I am truly grateful for the life I have been blessed to live, yet the hungry and homeless man tugs at my heart and raises many questions. As a follower of Jesus, how should I respond? Should I roll down my window and hand him some money? Would such a tangible act of well-intentioned benevolence truly help him? Should I pause to pray with him? Or stop and talk with him? Should I attempt to assist this man, perhaps transporting him to a local social service agency or a homeless shelter? What does it mean to love this neighbor of mine?

Jesus reminded his disciples that the poor would always be among them, yet even as material impoverishment is a perennial consequence of a broken world, we are called to neighborly love that cares for the poor among us. In an increasingly flattened, globalized world, what does it mean to love our materially impoverished neighbors—both global and local? What about the materially poor living in our own communities?[1] What about the working poor struggling in our cities, or those most vulnerable in our nation and throughout the globe? What is our responsibility both as individuals and as institutions like the local church?

WHAT IS POVERTY?

In order to care for the poor among us, we need to answer a fundamental question: What is poverty? What do we mean when we identify a neighbor as impoverished? Poverty is often defined in terms of falling below a particular threshold of individual or household income. While this material and monetized definition of poverty is helpful, from a Christian point of view it is not comprehensive enough. Brian Fikkert and Steve Corbett offer a helpful way forward. They rightly frame human impoverishment not merely in financial terms but fundamentally in relational categories. "Poverty is the result of relationships that do not work, that are not just, that are not for life, that are not harmonious or enjoyable. Poverty is the absence of shalom in all its meanings."[2]

When we think of human impoverishment, we must first and foremost recognize that poverty is a relational deficit. Poverty is lacking relationships that bring flourishing. This moves us beyond a reductionist, material view of the world, because no matter the level of our material wealth, we all are deeply impoverished. The pervasiveness of sin both on an individual and societal basis means that in a meaningful sense every human being is poor. None of us are fully flourishing as God designed us to flourish. Mother Teresa wisely observed the nonmaterial dimension of poverty in the West:

> In the West you have another kind of poverty, spiritual poverty. This is far worse. People do not believe in God, do not pray. People do not care for each other. You have the poverty of people who are dissatisfied with what they have, who do not know how to suffer, who give in to despair. This poverty of heart is often more difficult to relieve and defeat.[3]

Certainly there is a very real and important material dimension to human poverty, but we must not miss that our relational brokenness with God and our neighbor leads to loss of meaning, purpose, and hope. As economists who are committed to poverty alleviation around the globe, Fikkert and Corbett's research speaks loudly to those with ears to hear: "While poor people mention having a lack of material things, they tend to describe their condition in far more psychological terms. . . . Poor people typically talk [of poverty] in terms of shame, inferiority, powerlessness, humiliation, fear, hopelessness, depression, social isolation and voicelessness."[4] Because impoverishment extends beyond the lack of material resources, our comprehensive answer to human impoverishment must reach beyond the material dimension of human existence. If we want to fully address human impoverishment, we must probe the spiritual dimension, seeking restoration of our broken relationship with God.

THE GOSPEL AND POVERTY

Discussion of human impoverishment brings with it underlying assumptions about anthropology. Are humans basically good and in need of better education or greater enlightenment in order to flourish, or are humans fundamentally flawed and in need of being made new? How we understand the human condition will determine what solutions are offered for greater human flourishing. Theologian N. T. Wright points out the logical implications of an anthropology that asserts humanity's basic goodness. "We live in a world where politicians, media pundits, economists and even, alas, some late-blooming liberal theologians speak as if humankind is basically all right, the world is basically all right, and there's nothing we should make a fuss about."[5] Though this kind of anthropology might result in the establishment of initiatives or passing of laws designed to alleviate the effects of material poverty, it regularly fails to engage the deeper, most fundamental dimensions of human impoverishment.

When we see humans for who they truly are and the world as it truly is, I believe we should make a fuss about it. The hearts within us, the neighbors living next to us, and the world around us are one big, glorious mess. We are not as we ought to be, and the world is not as it ought to be. Jesus wept when he came face to face with his dear friend Lazarus's death, as he experienced personally the brokenness of the world he created and loves. The flowing tears of Jesus would lead him to a Roman cross, where he would shed his innocent blood as an atoning sacrifice for us. It was out of unfathomable love that Jesus left the throne room of God, with its inestimable riches, to take on human flesh and enter our broken world. Jesus became poor for our sake. Paul writes, "You know the grace of our Lord Jesus Christ, that though he was rich, yet for your sake he became poor, so that you by his poverty might become rich" (2 Cor 8:9). Even though we were alienated from God and desperately poor, Jesus intervened so that by grace we might become unimaginably rich in him.

The good news of the gospel is that though we are badly broken, we can be made new again. Jesus told Nicodemus that he needed to be born again. The apostle Paul points to the gospel as the answer to a sinful and flawed humanity in need, not merely of education or reformation, but of complete regeneration. "Therefore if any one is in Christ, he is a new creation. The old has passed away, behold, the new has come" (2 Cor 5:17). The gospel reminds us we are more broken than we realize, yet we are more loved than we have ever imagined. The gospel gives us a sure hope that by grace through faith in Christ our relationship with God can be reconciled and restored. Without our relationship with God being restored in Christ, no matter the degree of our material scarcity or abundance, we face the gravest human impoverishment imaginable, not only now but for all eternity.[6]

GOSPEL PROCLAMATION

We must not neglect or minimize human material impoverishment, but neighborly love compels us with the greatest sense of loving urgency to boldly share the good news. The power of the gospel is able to restore our neighbors' greatest impoverishment, a broken relationship with God. At the heart of poverty alleviation is the great need for reconciliation both with God and others. No private benevolence or government program, however noble and well crafted, can alter the very contours and affections of the fallen human heart. Only the gospel can accomplish this.

The apostle Paul grasped the gravity of the fallen and rebellious human condition. Paul understood both from revealed propositional truth as well as his own personal experience that only the gospel was capable of addressing and remedying our sinful and broken human condition. In his letter to the Romans, Paul, who took seriously the call to neighborly love, embraced his stewardship of living and proclaiming the gospel. Knowing the solution to the human sin condition, Paul transparently makes the point that he is both under obligation and eager to share the gospel. Paul understood humanity's greatest impoverishment was a spiritual impoverishment, and he was not ashamed to preach the gospel in response to that great need. "I am not ashamed of the gospel, for it is the power of God for salvation to everyone who believes, to the Jew first and also to the Greek" (Rom 1:16). If we understand poverty is first and foremost rooted in broken relationships, then the ultimate answer to human impoverishment is found in the transforming power of Jesus' death and resurrection, which not only restores our relationship with God but also makes possible our reconciliation with others, and will one day restore all relationships in the new heavens and new earth. If we are going to embrace poverty alleviation with the seriousness it demands, we must embrace the gospel with all the hope it offers. If we truly care about poverty alleviation, gospel proclamation is not optional; it is essential.

GOD'S HEART FOR THE POOR

The gospel not only needs to be proclaimed with our mouths, it must be embedded in our hearts and incarnated in our lives. When we read the Holy Scriptures, God's tender heart for the poor is a continual refrain. Scripture often speaks of God's regard for the materially impoverished and the economically vulnerable. Ethicist and theologian Scott Rae makes the salient point, "The marginalized, vulnerable and oppressed occupy a special place in the heart of God, because they have only him as their defender and advocate."[7]

It is not incidental that God's heart for the poor was codified in the Old Testament law. God's covenant people were cautioned against having hardened their hearts toward the poor. They were also urged to have open hands toward the poor. "If among you, one of your brothers should become poor, in any of your towns within your land that the LORD your God is giving you, you shall not harden your heart or shut your hand against your poor brother, but you shall open your hand to him and lend him sufficient for his need, whatever that may be" (Deut 15:7-8). The Old Testament law included provisions that enabled the poor not only to have access to benevolent neighbors but also to possess the dignity of providing for their own basic needs. In an agrarian economy, this provision was called "gleaning," and we observe its down-to-earth practice in the beautiful story of a young Moabite woman.

A WOMAN NAMED RUTH

Against the backdrop of famine and family tragedy, a young widow named Ruth leaves her homeland of Moab and journeys to the homeland of her mother-in-law, Naomi. As both a foreigner and a woman, Ruth arrives in Bethlehem in a highly vulnerable state, both economically and personally. Though things could have gone from bad to worse for this refugee in a foreign country, a relative of Naomi, Boaz, recognizes Ruth's vulnerability and intervenes on her behalf. Boaz opens his heart and hands to Ruth. Boaz embodied the letter and spirit of the Old Testament law, using his economic power and influence to provide access and protection for Ruth. Boaz lets Ruth glean grain in his field, recognizing her need for immediate material provision. He also provided safety to Ruth, knowing that a poor woman and foreigner like herself might be vulnerable to physical or sexual abuse. It is hard to imagine the joy and peace Ruth must have felt when Boaz said to her, "Now, listen, my daughter, do not go to glean in another field or leave this one, but keep close to my young women. Let your eyes be on the field that they are reaping and go after them. Have I not charged the young men not to touch you? And when you are thirsty, go to the vessels and drink what the young men have drawn" (Ruth 2:8-9).

Though Ruth's story begins in loss, desperation, and economic vulnerability, it ends with great blessing and redemption. The actions of Boaz not only reflect God's heart for the poor but also present to us timeless wisdom for poverty alleviation. Boaz's affirmation of Ruth's human dignity, provision of physical safety, and willingness to offer her access to productive work are instructive for us today.

Likewise, we must not miss the high value and esteemed importance of the poor in God's beautiful redemptive story. Ruth's story ends remarkably. The poor, foreign widow ultimately marries Boaz and eventually becomes the great-grandmother of King David. Boaz, the righteous kinsmen redeemer, anticipates the ultimate kinsmen redeemer, Jesus, who is born into the lineage of David centuries after Boaz shows neighborly love to Ruth.

JESUS AND THE POOR

In his death and resurrection, Jesus the Messiah provides the final solution for humanity's greatest poverty. However, we must also remember that Jesus himself demonstrated compassion and care for the materially poor throughout his earthly ministry. When Jesus spoke about his messianic mission, he often spoke of the poor. In his hometown of Nazareth, as he read the Isaiah scroll, Jesus identified himself as one bringing good news to the materially impoverished. "The Spirit of the Lord is upon me, / because he has anointed me / to proclaim good news to the poor" (Lk 4:18). And as John the Baptist languished in prison, having second thoughts about Jesus and his messianic mission, Jesus reassured John by informing him that all kinds of healing has occurred, and that "the poor have good news preached to them" (Mt 11:5). Jesus highlights the economic dimension of his messianic work alongside his physical healings.

Throughout the gospel, we see Jesus look on the multitudes with deep, heartfelt compassion, moved by those who were poor, weary, and sick. Our Lord told stories that gave dignity to the poor and elevated their status. A poignant example is a story Jesus told of the rich man and the poor man, Lazarus, whose disparate temporal circumstances in this life are highlighted to a hyperbolic extreme (Lk 16:19-31).[8] Jesus heightens his listeners' visceral response by portraying the rich man as indulging his opulent lifestyle with a cold and callous indifference to sick, hungry, and poor Lazarus, who sat by the rich man's gate each day. The rich man sees Lazarus, but only with his eyes and not with his heart. Even the dogs that roam the streets have more compassion for the poor man than the rich man does; they lick Lazarus's oozing sores to bring temporary relief. But the rich man remains indifferent.

To heighten the intrinsic value of the poor man, Jesus gives a name to this poor beggar, which is very unique within his parabolic teaching. In the midst of his ongoing suffering, Lazarus exhibits a gentle and patient soul, while the rich man reflects a prideful, self-absorbed, unrepentant heart. With this heart-tugging story, Jesus attempts to get the attention of the cold-hearted pharisaical religious leaders, who have bought into false conclusions that material wealth signifies God's blessing and material impoverishment serves as a rightful punishment for sin.

New Testament scholar Kenneth Bailey makes the compelling case that Jesus' parable of the rich man and Lazarus teaches several heart-changing themes, including the corrupting potential of material wealth.

> Wealth, be it little or much, is not condemned in Scripture. What is criticized is the failure to see that all material possessions belong to God. We are merely stewards of his treasures. The parable reflects the corrupting, blinding potential of wealth and is critical of the socially irresponsible wealthy. The rich man used his resources for his own self-indulgent living. He cared nothing about his God, his staff or the needy in his community.[9]

Jesus also highlighted sacrificial generosity toward the poor, showcasing the giving of a humble widow, who gave all the money she had to the work of the temple. Indeed, Jesus identifies so closely with the materially impoverished that he says when we care for the poor, it is as if we are caring for him.

Following in Jesus' footsteps, the New Testament writers continue to amplify God's heart for the poor. One of the compelling evidences of the outpouring of the Holy Spirit at Pentecost was how the gospel opened hearts and hands to those who were materially needy. Not out of coercion or forced distribution, but out of generous hearts of neighborly love, the early church met many material needs. "They were selling their possessions and belongings and distributing the proceeds to all, as any had need" (Acts 2:45). The New Testament writer James captures the early church's heart for the marginalized and vulnerable, emphasizing that true Christian faith has at its heart concern for the poor: "Religion that is pure and undefiled before God the Father is this: to visit orphans and widows in their affliction, and to keep oneself unstained from the world" (Jas 1:27).

The apostle Paul's concern for the poor was consistently on his heart and often on his tongue. In his farewell address, Paul urged the Ephesian elders to work hard, stay generous, and be eager to help the economically vulnerable. Defending his apostolic gospel mission to the Gentile world, Paul affirms his eagerness to care for the poor. While Paul preached and planted churches, he also took up monetary offerings to care for the materially impoverished in the Jerusalem church (Rom 15:25-28).[10] Paul's earnest appeal for generous giving to those who are underresourced, particularly to members of other local churches, suggests the goodness of striving for economic equity for all.

Paul does not advocate a coercive ecclesiastical or government redistribution of income or wealth, but rather seems to suggest that people who have been transformed by the gospel should embrace wise efforts to encourage less economic disparity and more economic equality. Writing to a financially advantaged church at Corinth, Paul says, "I do not mean that others should be eased and you burdened, but that as a matter of fairness, your abundance at the present time should supply their need, so that their abundance may supply your need, that there may be fairness" (2 Cor 8:13-14). In a time of increasing wealth disparity, both within the church and outside the church, Paul's words should be carefully pondered. How should the principle of equity or fairness inform our lifestyles, philanthropic efforts, and public policy? How does equity and fairness play a role in our free-market economy as we seek the flourishing of all people?

When we take a closer look at the extensive biblical teaching that calls for open hearts and hands toward the materially under-resourced, we realize God's heart for the poor is expressed not merely in acts of benevolent charity but also in providing oppor-tunity for work and productive engagement in the economy. Whether the poor are part of a local faith community or not, in common grace we are called to empower, strengthen, and protect the vulnerable in society.

BARRIERS TO POVERTY ALLEVIATION

For us to engage wisely in caring for the poor, we must deal with some common barriers to poverty alleviation. These barriers affect the heart, mind, and hands. When it comes to our understanding of and engagement with the materially poor, we may harbor wrongful attitudes, embrace misguided thinking, and live in cul-tural insularity.

Wrongful attitudes. If we come from more advantaged economic contexts, it is easy to assume a condescending attitude or patron-izing posture to those who are economically underresourced. From a perch of pride, we may look down at the poor, assuming they have significant personal problems, have led lazy and irresponsible lives, or simply are not too intelligent. We may even blame the poor for their plight, concluding that they have made their own mess and ought to sort it out themselves. Corbett and Fikkert describe this prideful attitudinal barrier, which does a great deal of damage in poverty alleviation efforts:

> One of the biggest problems in many poverty-alleviation ef-forts is that their design and implementation exacerbates the poverty of being of the economically rich—their

god-complexes—and the poverty of being of the economically poor—their feelings of inferiority and shame. The way we act toward the economically poor often communicates—albeit unintentionally—that we are superior and they are inferior. In the process we hurt the poor and ourselves.[11]

Corbett and Fikkert rightly call us to approach the under-resourced with a posture of Christlike humility and hopefulness, recognizing God is very much at work in poor communities.[12] Though we might have stronger educational backgrounds, more monetized wealth, or greater societal access, we have much to learn and gain from our engagement with our materially poor neighbors. In fact, the economically poor can be and often are some of our best teachers. The New Testament writer James reminds us that the economically poor are often spiritually rich. Regardless of our economic context, as fellow image bearers of God, we come to the common table of broken humanity, bringing a contribution for the blessing and enrichment of others.

Growing up in an underresourced, single-parent home, there were many places and spaces where I felt the sadness and shame of my impoverishment. But at one particular community gathering, those feelings melted away. In my rural community, the crescendo of summer was the Independence Day celebration hosted at our local church. Along with a competitive softball tournament, fun games, and booming fireworks, there was always a grand potluck dinner. As a young boy, I had never seen so much food. Table after table presented the most scrumptious fare. Mom, along with a host of other ladies from a variety of economic contexts in the community, brought something for the common table. It didn't matter what kind of food was contributed or how much of it there was, we all ate to our fill and then some. On that day, I didn't feel poor. As I watched the fireworks fill the starlit sky, somehow everything seemed good in the world, and everyone in our community was flourishing.

The image of a common table should shape our engagement with the materially impoverished. There are no vertical relationships at a common table, only horizontal interactions. As image bearers of God, humans are to extend neighborly love on a level playing field—person to person, not helper to helped.

Misguided thinking. We not only need to confront wrongful attitudes toward the poor, we also need to discern misguided thinking about the poor. One of the most prevalent misconceptions we hold toward material poverty is that its causes and solutions can be easily discerned through a simplistic lens. We tend to think that if we could somehow get the right government policies in place, more aggressively address mental health issues, alter generational patterns, fortify marriages and family life, or create more economic opportunity, then the challenges of poverty would be solved. In reality, poverty is quite complex. Human impoverishment, like human flourishing, brings with it a historical narrative and a host of contributing factors. This is not to say that all poverty contributors are of equal importance or need the same degree of focus at any particular time in any particular context. But a host of historical, individual, institutional, and systemic factors play a contributing role in human impoverishment.

Pastor Tim Keller astutely confronts the misguided notion of simplicity when it comes to poverty alleviation: "Poverty, therefore, is seen in the Bible as a very complex phenomenon. Several factors are usually intertwined. Poverty cannot be eliminated simply by personal initiative or by merely changing the tax structure. Multiple factors are usually interactively present in the life of a poor family."[13]

Short-term solutions. On the heels of misguided, simplistic thinking about poverty alleviation often comes wrongful notions concerning short-term solutions. We live in a fast-paced, nano-second world, where instant access, quick solutions, and immediate gratification bombard us. Somehow, because we can retrieve information in the blink of an eye or solve a computer glitch in minutes, we are prone to think poverty too can be solved quickly and conclusively. We may look for the latest poverty alleviation idea and convince ourselves it is *the* silver bullet. We may naively buy into the latest pied piper politician declaring they will care for the poor by bringing economic fairness and equality, taxing the rich, and issuing more and more government benefits to the materially impoverished.

Short-term, quick-fix solutions to poverty may alleviate guilt or overcome initial inertia, but they do not work when it comes to addressing the complex and systemic dimensions of poverty. Often, quick fixes do more harm than good.[14] In many cases, impoverished people and the underresourced, unsafe neighborhoods they inhabit are the result of entrenched individual and generational patterns, family deterioration, government policy, systemic injustice, and the lack of economic opportunity. Corbett and Fikkert speak with a needed bluntness: "Therein resides the problem of many poverty alleviation efforts: the North American need for speed undermines the slow process needed for lasting and effective long-run development."[15] Taking poverty alleviation seriously will mean we keep a long horizon in view. Effective poverty alleviation not only requires a ton of wisdom and massive collaboration, it also takes time. Poverty alleviation is a long-term effort. The sizeable challenges and often discouraging obstacles of poverty alleviation should shatter any bubble of quick-fix idealism.

More money. Another common misconception related to the alleviation of material poverty is to assume that what is needed most is more money. While inadequate financial resources are a critical aspect of poverty, having more dollars does not necessarily move people out of poverty. Increased money, whether it comes from private benevolence or government programs, can be spent unwisely and foster dependence instead of enhancing personal dignity, encouraging personal responsibility, or paving the way for sustainable wealth creation. One of the things I have learned as I have collaborated with pastors, who daily serve the rural and urban poor, is the vital importance of not just providing money but also opening doors of access and economic opportunity for the poor.

When it comes to economic support, we must realize that what the underresourced need more is not so much money donations as the opening of doors of access and influence, so that they might no longer be shut out of economic or educational systems. Andy Crouch makes this important point as he speaks of the blind spot many of us who enjoy greater access to cultural influence and power tend to have. "Privilege is a special kind of power. It is the form of power that requires no effort. Indeed, only in unusual circumstances do we become conscious of it at all. Most of the time privilege just works on behalf of those who have it, never making the slightest demands on them."[16] While cultural privilege is a gracious gift and should not be a source of guilt or self-loathing, love of God and neighbor compels us to steward wisely what we have been given. Jesus reminds us that much will be required from those who have been given much (Lk 12:48). Any vocational authority, cultural influence, or other form of power we might yield should be used to open doors to those who have found the doors of education, influence, and opportunity barred shut. It is one of the most important poverty alleviation strategies we have to tangibly demonstrate our neighborly love.

Cultural insularity. Cultural insularity is another big barrier to poverty alleviation, because it blinds us to many of our poorest neighbors. The poor among us are in many different places and have many diverse faces. The materially poor and economically vulnerable live in rural areas, suburbs, and city centers.[17] There are working poor, nonworking poor, homeless, elderly, orphans, foster care children, refugees, legal immigrants, and illegal immigrants. The problem is that our own cultural isolation often prevents us from seeing or encountering the poor among us in a regular, meaningful, or personal way. We may feel indifferent to the plight of the poor, having convinced ourselves that the poor ought simply to pull themselves up by their own economic bootstraps. On the other hand, we may dismiss any personal responsibility in this aspect of neighborly love by placing poverty alleviation squarely on the shoulders of the government.

One of the dripping ironies of our Information Age is that we have such extraordinary access to our diverse global village, yet we often choose by our daily lifestyles to live in the comfortable enclaves of ghettoized familiarity. Rather than being aware of our local and global neighbors, we simply tune out much of the world. The barrier of cultural insularity may be amplified in commuter-driven, suburban living, but is not confined to suburban life. Cultural insularity is also prevalent in rural and center-city areas. Living insular and isolated lives is more the result of self-absorption than it is a consequence of the place we live or our socioeconomic status. In today's world we can choose to live, work, and play with people just like us—people who look like us, work in the same vocation as us, go to the same schools that we do, and have the same economic lifestyle we maintain. Cultural insularity not only blinds us to the needs of others, it also impoverishes us. Whether they are affluent or underresourced, cultural ghettos inevitably deprive us of relational richness.

STRANGERS IN OUR MIDST

I was reminded of my own impoverished cultural insularity when my wife, Liz, and I were introduced to an Iranian family who had been relocated to Kansas City from a refugee camp in Turkey. As Muslims who had converted to Christianity, Hossein, Marzia, and their son had experienced great persecution, leaving family, friends, and everything they owned when they fled from Iran to Turkey. After extensive interviews and two long years of waiting, Hossein and Marzia were selected by a United States government agency to start life over in America. Hossein and Marzia arrived in Kansas City with nothing but their warm smiles and the shirts on their backs. Upon their arrival, Hossein and Marzia needed access to medical care, an apartment to live in, language training, opportunities for employment, and new friends. The apartment they were assigned to was dark, dingy, and unfurnished. The neighborhood they were placed in was drug infested and crime ridden.

Our faith community welcomed Hossein and Marzia with open arms, loving them and assisting them in the process of becoming at home in a new country. My son Schaeffer helped them craft résumés, and Liz worked to open doors of access for employment. Our family grew to love and cherish our friendship with Hossein and Marzia. We learned much from them and were encouraged by the richness of their cultural traditions and vibrant Christian faith. In a transforming way, the blinding scales of our cultural insularity fell from our eyes. We became much more aware of the great vulnerability of refugees in our city and the sizeable personal and economic challenges they face every day. We also saw firsthand how the economically vulnerable need strong collaboration from the institutions of government, nonprofit agencies, for-profit businesses, and local faith communities to thrive.

Many of us need to take initiative and step outside of our comfortable bubble of cultural insularity. To love and learn from our neighbors, we must spend time with them. We need to be with them where they live. Jesus teaches the best way to bless the poor is to talk with, listen to, and love them. Jesus reached out to the poor first through conversation, affirming their worth as persons and seeing them through a holistic frame. As we endeavor to thoughtfully respond to the spiritual and material poverty of our neighbors, we must do the same. The call to neighborly love is a call to brave and empathetic engagement—a call that requires compassion, capacity, and a willingness to confront economic injustice.

10

ECONOMIC INJUSTICE

*The sin of injustice is defined in the Bible as the abuse
of power—abusing power by taking from others the good
things God intended for them, namely their life, liberty,
dignity, or the fruits of their love or their labor.*

GARY HAUGEN, *JUST COURAGE*

*Even though you offer me your burnt offerings
and grain offerings,
I will not accept them;
and the peace offerings of your fattened animals,
I will not look upon them.
Take away from me the noise of your songs;
to the melody of your harps I will not listen.
But let justice roll down like waters,
and righteousness like an ever-flowing stream.*

AMOS 5:22-24

I n his eye-opening book *Just Courage*, Gary Haugen recounts story
after story detailing the tragic injustices suffered by marginalized
and disadvantaged people around the globe. Of the many narratives

he presents, one story in particular has stuck with me. Haugen writes of Mary, a mother in Phnom Penh, Cambodia, whose daughter is abducted, transported to Thailand, and sold into sex slavery. Haugen describes Mary's utter devastation upon learning of her daughter's captivity, and he speaks of her desperate attempt to seek help from police. But when she turns to the authorities, Mary's cries of help are greeted by requests for bribes. Those charged with protecting her and her family seek financial gain instead of committing to pursue her daughter's captors. My heart sinks as I imagine Mary's horror and her feelings of frustration and helplessness—prompted both by her daughter's situation and by her own inability to intervene. Haugen offers a poignant window into the heartache of a broken mother. But I also know that Mary's heart isn't the only one that burns as a result of her daughter's brutal exploitation. God is watching, and his heart too aches as a result of this injustice.

Throughout Holy Scripture, we not only hear God's compassionate heartbeat for the poor and exploited, we also hear his righteous anger toward those who malign and take advantage of others. The Old Testament prophets speak out against all manner of injustice, yet they specifically decry exploitative economic behavior. The prophet Amos offers a rebuking lament to God's covenant people, who have ignored and abandoned the teachings of the Torah regarding the foreigner and the poor (Lev 19:33-35).[1] Amos points out how the poor are being "trampled on" through excessive taxation and the corruption of bribery. The moving image of the poor being stomped underfoot not only makes clear that Israel's leaders were abusing their power but also highlights the egregious ways in which the basic rights of the poor were being disregarded.[2] Amos also emphasizes that the injustice being perpetrated against the economically vulnerable was not an isolated case but a systemic reality. Amos describes a corrupt and rigged economic system of deceptive measurements, where inferior products were being sold at inflated prices for exorbitant profits (Amos 8:4-8).[3] This systemic injustice perpetually advantaged the rich and powerful, while disadvantaging the poor.

Throughout his prophetic writing, Amos repeatedly refers to "the gate," which was the powerful center of economic transactions within a community. In contemporary parlance, we might see many parallels between a city's gate and a stock exchange or online marketplace like eBay. The gates of our modern economy can promote human flourishing, or they can perpetuate economic injustice and hinder human flourishing.

Amos speaks with crystal clarity and unction, calling economic injustice evil and exhorting God's covenant people to repentance: "Hate evil, and love good, and establish justice in the gate" (Amos 5:15). Amos goes so far as to say that when God's people ignore injustice and fail to do justice, God despises their worship and refuses to listen to them (Amos 5:21-24).

The psalmist echoes God's deep concern for justice for the poor.

Give justice to the weak and the fatherless;
   maintain the right of the afflicted and the destitute.
Rescue the weak and the needy;
   deliver them from the hand of the wicked. (Ps 82:3-4)

While there are many kinds of evil perpetrated by the more powerful against the less powerful, the abuse of economic power is seen by the psalmist as heinously wicked. Few barriers of poverty alleviation are more challenging yet more crucial to address than economic injustice.

PROPHETS AND PROFITS

I am compelled by the very nature of my vocational calling not only to offer pastoral care to the hurting but also to provide a prophetic voice for the many who face injustice—the vulnerable and voiceless.

Yet as a spokesperson for God, a prophetic voice must not only point out the errors of injustice but also offer better ways forward for the flourishing of all. In speaking to those in the for-profit world, my prophetic message is not that economic profits do not matter, they clearly do. Rather, it is to warn that economic profits can come to matter too much and can blind us to our stewardship of the common good.[4] When the idolatry of power and economic greed captures the human heart, it is only a matter of time until the indiscriminate shrapnel of injustice does great damage. At the heart of the matter, injustice is a matter of the heart.

Not only do unjust economic systems that hinder opportunity and access to economic flourishing need changing, human hearts need changing. Gospel proclamation and advocacy for justice go hand in hand. Pastors must advocate a neighborly love of increased compassion as well as growing economic capacity. We must promote principles of timeless economic wisdom articulated in Scripture, while encouraging their individual and systemic implementation. Andy Crouch rightly asserts, "Justice is about much more than relieving suffering—it is about a vision of human flourishing."[5] The prophet Amos does not merely point out the presence of egregious economic injustice, he also paints a picture of a better and more flourishing future: "Let justice roll down like waters, and righteousness like an ever-flowing stream" (Amos 5:24).

In the pages that follow, I outline the broad contours of a few current realities in which pastoral advocacy for economic justice is desperately needed. I am not endeavoring to present an exhaustive list, identifying every area in which thoughtful and faithful Christ-followers ought to be engaged. Rather, my prayer is that the descriptions of these injustices might stir our hearts, capture our imaginations, and serve to spark neighborly love in the various contexts that we inhabit.

Preying on the poor. One of the most challenging and complex economic realities faced by many of our neighbors who live paycheck to paycheck is finding financial resources to cover immediate and unexpected expenses. To address this need, a profitable, multibillion-dollar payday loan industry has emerged in our free-market economy. In an *Atlantic* article titled "Payday Lending: Will Anything Better Replace It?" Bethany McLean provides a helpful window into the troubling, yet complex world of this industry.

Payday lending organizations serve more than nineteen million American households each year. The typical payday loan is about $350 and must be repaid within two weeks. In theory, these small loans provide some cash liquidity until the next paycheck arrives. A single interest fee, usually around $15, is charged per $100 borrowed. This charge, when annualized, makes the interest rate levied by payday lenders an astounding 400 percent. Yet this is hardly the worst of it. Many times, working poor borrowers cannot afford to pay back their loan within the standard two-week window. So the outstanding amount is rolled over and more fees are added. Like a snowball gaining speed and mass as it heads downhill, the interest costs continue to skyrocket as the already poor borrower becomes poorer because of these debt traps.[6]

Advocates of payday loans suggest that the high interest charges exacted on the working poor are not unfair because payday loan operations provide a necessary service for cash liquidity. Payday loan companies also point out the high risk of default requires the high reward of high interest. Others point out that the profit margins of the payday loan industry are similar to other industries and are not excessive. Yet, in a time of historically low interest rates for more materially advantaged citizens, the high interest rates exacted by payday loan companies on the poorest citizens seem increasingly problematic.

The payday loan industry is a telling example of the kinds of complex and systemic economic challenges the poor among us face. While the payday loan system is viable from an economic point of view, from a moral perspective I do not believe it is an acceptable answer to meet the liquidity needs of the working poor. This status quo must be challenged, and a better way forward needs to be championed. Does the current, unacceptable payday lending reality call Christians and Christian leaders to work for a better solution? What might a local church do to provide other alternatives for the working poor who face unexpected expenses? How do we wisely come alongside a growing number of people who are living paycheck to paycheck with no financial margin for emergencies? Looking for a better solution than the shortsighted, Band-Aid of payday lending, Bethany McLean concludes, "The problem isn't just that people who desperately need a $350 loan can't get it at an affordable rate, but that a growing number of people need that loan in the first place."[7]

In addition to payday lending, other economic activities disproportionately hurt the poor. While gambling and lotteries offer the hope of instantly moving from rags to riches, the odds of winning are gargantuan. Yet many economically underresourced individuals feel they have little to lose and much to gain by a potential win, so they spend their limited resources on the slim hope of economic salvation through a jackpot drawing. The lottery serves as a lucrative tax coffer for the state, a tax that the poor cannot afford to pay.[8]

Another regressive tax that disproportionately affects the poor is state sales tax levied on food, clothing, and other items necessary for everyday living. While subsidies are available in the form of food stamps, in the state where I reside both the affluent and the impoverished pay the same sales-tax rate at the grocery store. This too is an unjust economic reality that needs to change.

Gender discrimination in the form of lower pay for women who perform the same work as men also hurts the poor. Similarly, the economic injustice of crony capitalism reminds the poor and powerless that the system is rigged in favor of the politically connected. This not only sows seeds of cynicism, it also evaporates hope that the poor can work hard and experience greater economic opportunity.

Racial discrimination. While racism lurks in the broken depths of every human heart, not all racism has had and continues to have such a negative impact as the individual and institutional racism perpetrated against African Americans in the United States. Much has been written about the systemic racism inherent in our nation's historic enslavement of African Americans, as well as the injustice perpetuated by subsequent Jim Crow laws. My purpose is not to delve into the agonizing depths of racial injustice but rather to heighten the awareness of the deep wounds and economic challenges that have existed and continue to exist for many African Americans.

Kansas City is the place I call home. The "City of Fountains," as it is often called, is a wonderful place to live—at least for me. It is a different story for some dear neighbors. Indeed, many African Americans disproportionately live in parts of the city where crime is rampant, education is lacking, housing is substandard, nutritious food is absent, and job opportunities are virtually nonexistent. While there are many contributing factors to such visible lack of flourishing, the tragic racist history of our city has played a big role. One of the chief developers of Kansas City was J. C. Nichols, who shaped and planned some of the city's most affluent neighborhoods. Nichols guaranteed that African Americans would be prevented from living in any of his communities by authoring restrictive housing covenants that kept African Americans from owning or occupying properties within his communities.[9] Such a practice is absolutely evil.

Because of the courage of leaders like Dr. Martin Luther King Jr. and the civil rights movement, significant progress has been made in providing African Americans access to educational and economic opportunities. Still, the enduring effect of decades of economic disenfranchisement in African American communities is compelling.

The long-lasting consequences of systemic racism linger, and formidable obstacles of discrimination remain.[10] Leveling the playing field of educational and economic opportunity for African Americans is not optional for those who embrace the gospel and seek to live out the restorative justice it calls us to pursue.[11] When we confront economic injustice seriously, we must take racial reconciliation seriously. Pastor Timothy Keller gives the clarion call for the church to comprehensively care for the poor: "Doing justice in poor communities includes direct relief, individual development, community development, racial reconciliation, and social reform."[12]

As we seek to address the barrier of racial discrimination, it will require a renewed spirit of humility, understanding, and forgiveness.[13] The local church can be a faithful presence that brings peace to a community. Indeed, the church has been supernaturally empowered and given the ongoing responsibility to be a healing balm for deep social wounds, while actively seeking reconciliation with God and others.[14] Don Carson brings a wise perspective to the kind of loving posture churches must embrace if they are to be healing agents in a racially troubled time: "I doubt that we shall improve much in Christian circles until parties with the most power reflect a lot more than in the past on matters of justice, and the parties most victimized reflect a lot more than in the past on forgiveness."[15]

Human trafficking and slavery. One of the most heart-arresting injustices of our time is human trafficking and slavery. The scope of this moral and economic injustice must awaken our consciences and call us to wise action. Human trafficking and slavery is driven by economic forces of supply and demand, and takes many forms, including slave labor, sweatshops, and prostitution around the globe. In many cases, inadequate law, indifferent law enforcement, as well as massive political corruption protect and provide cover for the illegal human trafficking industry. Andy Crouch captures the egregious abuse of power and the magnitude of injustice: "Perhaps no statistic reminds us more graphically of the distortion of power in our world than this: there are twenty-one million slaves in the world today."[16] While human trafficking is a global problem, it is also a domestic problem. Sex slavery is all too prevalent in the cities and suburbs of America. We must open our eyes to the poor among us who are being enslaved and exploited for economic gain.

Global poverty. Neighborly love calls us to seek the flourishing of our neighbors—both local and global. Like all poverty, global poverty is a complex reality. An approach that has been common in addressing global poverty is foreign aid, in which wealthier nations give massive amounts of material resources to less wealthy nations. Economists Corbett and Fikkert describe the lack of effectiveness of this poverty alleviation strategy: "Despite an estimated $2.3 trillion in foreign aid dispensed from Western nations during the post-World War II era, more than 2.5 billion people, approximately 40 percent of the world population still live on less than two dollars per day. . . . Yes there has been progress in the global fight against poverty, but the 'bang for the buck' has been appallingly low."[17]

Though foreign aid has its place in global poverty alleviation, pastor Rick Warren offers nuanced thoughts on global poverty alleviation, warning against government solutions as well as misguided Christian humanitarian programs that often create dependency, rob people of dignity, and stifle initiative. He writes, "The biblical way to help people rise out of poverty is through wealth creation, not wealth redistribution. For lasting results, we must offer the poor a hand up, not merely a hand out. You spell long-term poverty reduction, 'j-o-b-s.' Training and tools liberate people. Trade, not aid, builds the prosperity of nations."[18]

Having seen the limitations as well as detrimental effects of foreign aid on poorer nations, more systemic and cultural approaches are being taken by governments. Private philanthropic efforts are also joining the fight against global poverty. Gary Haugen, who leads the International Justice Mission, has made a strong case that global poverty alleviation must address the safety needs of the poor, who face the ever-present threat of violence.[19] Haugen points out that the lack of protection of the poor through inadequate law enforcement and corrupt government officials must be addressed for the poor to thrive. Additionally, it has been demonstrated that free markets are vital catalysts for moving poorer nations into greater economic prosperity.[20] The cultivation of virtue and economically conducive values, alongside increasing health in institutions, plays a vital role in the economic growth and flourishing of a nation. "The cultural values of a nation determine what kind of economic system it adopts, what kind of laws and policies the government enacts, whether corruption is tolerated, whether freedoms are protected, and what kind of goals individuals set for their personal lives."[21]

MOVING FORWARD

Human impoverishment is truly complex. Yet its complexity must not paralyze us or lead us to passivity. Whether they live next to us, in another part of our city, or in another part of the globe, we must share God's heart and be God's hands for our economically vulnerable neighbors. We must also remember that human impoverishment is first a relational poverty. No matter our economic context, we are all relationally poor, and the gospel gives us hope for reconciliation with God and our neighbors. The gospel calls us to a neighborly love that nurtures a life of economic flourishing for ourselves and for others. To alleviate poverty, we will need to seek the Holy Spirit's empowerment and take a long-term perspective.

One church that has embraced a more comprehensive understanding of poverty and a more robust response to poverty alleviation is Fort McKinley United Methodist Church in Dayton, Ohio. Worship and community development coordinator Rusty Eshleman took on the task of moving the church's community outreach strategy from being focused on relief to being characterized by economic development. He started a six-week "Good Neighbor" class to help introduce church members to thoughtful perspectives on engagement with the poor. This new thinking resulted in new action. To address community members' need for jobs, the church launched GED classes and a "Jobs for Life" program that pursued long-term solutions to economic impoverishment instead of quick fixes. Now, a "Neighborhood Allies" team has been established, and economic flourishing is taking root—all because the church embraced the gospel call to care for the poor, and recognized that a loving response would seek to meet immediate needs as well as long-term self-sustainability for the underresourced.

In the spirit of the prophet Micah, let us roll up our sleeves and do justice, love kindness, and walk humbly with God (Mic 6:8). We can and must make a difference. We can partner with God and with others to rebuild the spiritual and economic ruins of our neighborhoods and our cities.

11

REBUILDING THE RUINS

A vocation is not found by looking within and finding
your passion. It is found by looking without
and asking what life is asking of us.

DAVID BROOKS, *THE ROAD TO CHARACTER*

And they said to me, "The remnant there in the province
who had survived the exile is in great trouble and shame. The wall
of Jerusalem is broken down, and its gates are destroyed by fire."

As soon as I heard these words, I sat down and wept
and mourned for days, and I continued fasting
and praying before the God of heaven.

NEHEMIAH 1:3-4

t was the winter of 444 BC. Nehemiah, a trusted adviser to the
Persian king Artaxerxes, found himself in a place of privilege
and power. Though he was Jewish and not Persian, the brilliance
of his mind, the strength of his character, and his gifts of leadership had catapulted Nehemiah to a top governmental job in the
most powerful nation of the world. In the midst of a demanding

work schedule, he must have paused at times to reflect on how far he had come and on the many ways life had been good to him. I wonder if he had any idea that life would soon ask something of him.

When an envoy of his countrymen arrived at the citadel in Susa, Nehemiah learned that his people were living in ruins. The great city of Jerusalem had stagnated and was in shambles, and its formerly great gates had not been rebuilt. From his place in the halls of Persian luxury and power, Nehemiah faced a big decision. Would he dismiss the downfall of a neighborhood far away as somebody else's concern, or would he take some sort of action? Would the information he'd learned implicate him with greater responsibility? Or would he avoid the responsibility that accompanies knowledge?

The prophet Jeremiah had told the exiles to seek the welfare of Babylon, but what about the welfare of Jerusalem? What was Nehemiah's responsibility to those in Jerusalem who were languishing? As a follower of the God of Abraham, Isaac, and Jacob, what did neighborly love require of him?

When it comes to the rubble and ruin of our world, we too are implicated because of what we know. Neighborly love requires that we wisely and intentionally integrate faith, work, and economics for the glory of God and the good of the world. I believe the book of Nehemiah points us in this important direction. Nehemiah helps us not only see our responsibility to promote the flourishing of both our local and global neighbors, but also provides needed guidance as we seek to enhance human flourishing and rebuild the ruins of our broken cities and society.

Nehemiah takes a comprehensive and holistic approach, showing us the wisdom-paved path to neighborly love leading us forward in both compassion and capacity. Theologian Miroslav

Volf particularly calls out Christian leaders to courageously step up and rebuild the ruins in our cultural moment.

> That, I think, is today's most fundamental challenge for theologians, priests, and ministers, and Christian laypeople: to really mean that the presence and activity of the God of love, who can make us love our neighbors as ourselves, is our hope and the hope of the world—that this God is the secret of our flourishing as persons, cultures and interdependent inhabitants of a single globe.[1]

In the book of Nehemiah we find a wise and principled way forward for pastors and Christian leaders who, out of the overflow of their love of God and neighbor, seek to enhance human flourishing and rebuild the ruins of sin-stained, broken cities and disintegrated social order. Nehemiah's writing and example offer encouragement and instruction to Christian leaders and faith communities who take seriously the call to neighborly love through the conduit of faith, work, and economic integration. Specifically, Nehemiah suggests that the huge task of rebuilding broken communities begins when we first see the need, and advances as we keep a Godward focus.

SEEING THE NEED

Upon hearing the sobering news about Jerusalem, Nehemiah's holy discontent drew him to his knees. Nehemiah's first priority was to pray, focusing not on the broken walls of Jerusalem but on the broken hearts of God's covenant people. Nehemiah's heartfelt prayer to God on behalf of God's covenant people exhibits wise understanding. Nehemiah knew the greatest impoverishment confronting all humans is the poverty that accompanies a broken relationship with God. Nehemiah cries out to God, "We have acted very corruptly against you and have not kept the commandments, the statutes, and the rules that you commanded your servant Moses" (Neh 1:7). Nehemiah understood that underlying the ruin and rubble of a broken city was an even more perilous ruin—the remains of humanity's sin-stained, broken relationships with God. Nehemiah's prayer tells us he grappled first with his own woeful spiritual condition. He cries out to God for personal forgiveness: "Even I and my father's house have sinned" (Neh 1:6).

Nehemiah begins where we must begin, by seeing a community's most fundamental need as a spiritual one. Without a restored relationship with God, no individual, community, or city will fully flourish. Without the spiritual insight and empowerment prayer brings, rebuilding the ruins of a community or a city is a mere dream. If anyone should grasp this truth, pastors and Christian leaders should. But tragically, our leadership passions and prayerless priorities often say something vastly different. Prayer is where we must begin, and it must permeate all we do.

As Nehemiah contemplates the dire situation of his homeland, he has no messiah complex. Nehemiah was intimately aware that he was a broken image bearer and covenant breaker, in desperate need of the mercy and forgiveness of God. His dependence on God led him to see his great need for supernatural empowerment for the task ahead: "O Lord, let your ear be attentive to the prayer of your servant, and to the prayer of your servants who delight to fear your name, and give success to your servant today, and grant him mercy in the sight of this man" (Neh 1:11). Without God's favor, Nehemiah was sure to fail.

After seeking God in prayer, Nehemiah put a plan together to rebuild the ruins of Jerusalem. Empowered by the Spirit, Nehemiah courageously presented his plan to King Artaxerxes. Remarkably, Nehemiah was given a green light to leave his Persian post and to go and rebuild the ruins of Jerusalem. Nehemiah not only bathed the broken ruins of Jerusalem in prayer, he also made his way to his homeland to see things for himself. He must have felt overwhelmed by the massive need he witnessed with his own eyes. Trudging through tons of rubble and decades of disintegration, he was greeted by neglect and tragedy at every turn. Inspecting broken wall after broken wall, Nehemiah must have been tempted to pack up and head back to Persia. Seeing the need through the eyes of faith, however, Nehemiah stayed, moving into this badly broken neighborhood.

ONE BRICK AT A TIME

Like Nehemiah, Chris Jehle grew up in a flourishing community, but he and his wife, Tammy, chose to move to a very broken neighborhood. The Oak Park, Ivanhoe, Palestine, and Santa Fe neighborhoods of Kansas City's east side did not always lie in ruin. These neighborhoods were once prosperous and flourishing. But years of neglect changed things dramatically. Substandard housing, deficient schools, high unemployment, medical care inaccessibility, and high rates of crime ravaged these neighborhoods, leaving residents searching for hope. Most at risk were children and youth, who were often unable to overcome the broken homes, educational insufficiencies, inadequate job skills, gun violence, illegal drug abuse, and sexual pressures they confronted daily. Seeing the ruin and rubble of these broken Kansas City neighborhoods, Chris and Tammy knew they were implicated. What did neighborly love require of them? What would it mean to truly love this neighborhood? What would it take for these neglected places to flourish again?

Galvanizing support from mission-minded local churches like Christ Community and from business and civic leaders, a Christian-centered gathering space called the Hope Center was birthed. In two decades of mission, the Hope Center has taken a comprehensive approach to rebuilding the ruins of this broken neighborhood. Hope Leadership Academy opened its doors, offering excellent education and espousing a bold mission of developing urban youth into world-class leaders. College preparation and job skill training are a vital part of its curriculum. A local church was planted in the neighborhood to provide spiritual community and Christian character formation. New homes have been built in collaboration with organizations like Habitat for Humanity, and a good deal of substandard housing has been remodeled. A sustainable community garden was established in order to counter the reality of poor nutrition, which is common in urban food deserts. The many flowers and abundant fresh produce in the community garden add beauty and affirm the dignity of community members who plant, cultivate, and harvest its nutritious food. The lack of accessible medical care in the neighborhood is being addressed by a clinic called the Hope Family Care Center. In addition to providing medical care to the sick, the Care Center focuses a great deal of energy on prenatal care and preventive medicine.

The Hope Center's empowering story demonstrates the strategic role a local church like Christ Community can play in rebuilding the ruins of a broken neighborhood one brick at a time. Rebuilding the ruins of a broken neighborhood is a long-term collaborative effort. It takes endurance, perseverance and regular doses of hope. Significant progress has been made in Kansas City's east side through the Hope Center's institutional efforts, but it never would have been realized without the Spirit-opened eyes of Chris and Tammy Jehle, who saw the dire need of a neighborhood and like Nehemiah concluded they were personally implicated in the task of causing it to flourish.

Steven Garber helps us wrestle with an important question. Can we truly know the world with all its brokenness and messiness and still love it? He reminds us we need "to learn to see—to see ourselves implicated in history, to see that we share a common vocation, to care not only for our own flourishing, but for the flourishing of the world."[2]

With so much rubble and ruin, will we as pastors and Christian leaders avoid the hopelessness of a corroding cynicism or the discouragement of a paralyzing pessimism? Will we see the world as it truly is and love it as it presently exists with a hopeful realism for what it can be? I believe we can, but to do so we must keep a Godward focus.

KEEPING A GODWARD FOCUS

Though Nehemiah waded knee deep in the rubble of ruin, from beginning to end, he walked before an Audience of One. Peppered throughout the book of Nehemiah are reminders of God's constant presence, protection, and provision. Nehemiah was vigilant in keeping a Godward focus. When Nehemiah went before the king to request an extended leave of absence, he sent up a quick prayer. After the king granted Nehemiah's request we read Nehemiah's confident assertion of God's favor, "the good hand of my God was upon me" (Neh 2:8). When Nehemiah faces criticism about rebuilding the ruins, he says, "The God of heaven will make us prosper" (Neh 2:20). When discouragement and fear of opposition set in, he exhorts the workers to "Remember the Lord, who is great and awesome" (Neh 4:14). Throughout the rebuilding process, Nehemiah interjects brief prayers, reminding God of his faithful service: "Remember for my good, O my God, all that I have done for this people" (Neh 5:19). Nehemiah concludes his book, "Remember me, O my God, for good" (Neh 13:31).

If we are to embrace true neighborly love like Nehemiah did, then we must anchor our own lives and church mission in a Godward direction. This will not only mean relying on God's constant protection and provision, but also embracing Jesus' economy of grace.

JESUS' ECONOMY OF GRACE

The word *grace* makes us think of many things. We like grace. We even sing about it: "Amazing grace how sweet the sound . . ." Yet if we would be entirely transparent, there are times when grace troubles us, particularly when it is extended to those we might deem unworthy. In those circumstances, grace seems anything but amazing.

Grace may not always be *our* way, but it is always *God's* way. In Matthew's Gospel, Jesus tells a story about a landowner who had a vineyard. This owner goes into town to hire workers at five different times in one day. He hired workers at 6 a.m., 9 a.m., noon, 3 p.m., and 5 p.m. Quitting time was around 6.

Jesus' first-century context may be unfamiliar to us. In our twenty-first-century economy, employers usually don't hire workers for only one day. In the first century, however, day laborers were typically hired first thing in the morning. Why then in Jesus' story does the vineyard owner keep going back for more workers? Was he a foolish owner or a poor planner? Not at all. It is because the good and gracious employer wanted every worker to have a job.[3] This owner had compassion for those who had waited for work all day, but ultimately found no way to productively contribute.

It shouldn't surprise us that Jesus told a story embedded in first-century economic life. Remember, the majority of Jesus' time on earth was spent working in a small business. In the Gospels, Jesus is described as a craftsman carpenter, which may mean that he had skills in stone cutting as well as in woodworking (see Mk 6:1-4). As a young businessperson, Jesus may have hired some day laborers to help him complete his work. His story affirms the goodness of the marketplace, upholds the dignity of work, and emphasizes the importance of economic life.

We must see, however, that Jesus places primary focus in this story not on the workers who are hired but on the employer who hires them. Jesus highlights that the landowner extends grace to all the workers in his acts of hiring. These multiple extensions of economic grace are designed to teach us this truth: The ultimate bottom line in the economy of Jesus is grace. Grace is the kingdom currency. You can't get very far without it. Economics is often seen as the allocation of scarce resources, but in Jesus' economy there is no scarcity of grace. No matter the time, place, or circumstances, God's grace is always available.

Thomas Friedman makes the case that rapid globalization has created a flattening effect in the twenty-first century, leveling the playing field of economic opportunity.[4] Likewise, in Jesus' story we see that the currency of grace has a moral flattening effect. Grace is available to everyone, which is precisely why we call it amazing. But Jesus' story takes a surprising turn. As the sun sets and the time comes for the vineyard owner to pay his workers, the owner chooses to pay those workers who arrived last first, and those who arrived first last. He also gives each the exact same amount. Jesus makes it crystal clear that the owner of the vineyard is deliberate in wanting those who had worked all day to see the grace he extends to those who worked for only an hour.

Jesus particularly focuses our attention on the contrast between those workers who arrived at the first hour and those who arrived at the eleventh. Imagine a worker who had labored twelve hours and a worker who had labored one being paid the same wage. It seems almost preposterous, doesn't it? Not only did the first workers labor eleven hours more than those who arrived at the end of the day, they also toiled during the scorching midday heat.

Not surprisingly, the first-hour workers are irate. It all seems so unfair. Certainly a protest calling for equal pay for equal work would be warranted. Indeed, that principle is rightly woven into our labor laws. But while equal pay for equal work is good in our economy, in Jesus' grace economy, fairness is not the currency of highest value. Grace is not opposed to well-intended effort, but it is opposed to meritorious earning. Grace can never be earned. Grace doesn't balance the scales. Grace makes the scales of fairness fade into irrelevance. When it comes to what God requires from each of us, we all fail to measure up.

At first blush, the vineyard owner's actions seem downright scandalous. But Jesus wants us to see whose actions are truly scandalous. Is the scandalous grace of the employer most upsetting, or the scandalous ingratitude of the first workers? When they compare themselves to the eleventh-hour workers, the first-hour workers' perspective changes. Though they received the wages the owner agreed to pay them, they are frustrated that the owner offered the same amount to those who arrived later. Throughout the day, they believed they were earning their wage. In fact, they might even have thought they were doing the vineyard owner a favor; when in reality the vineyard owner was doing them a favor. The work they had been given was a gift of grace. The fact they had work at all was grace.

In Jesus' story, only the first-hour workers grumble and complain, not the third-, the sixth-, or the ninth-hour workers. The third-, sixth-, and ninth-hour workers did not compare themselves to the eleventh-hour workers. Instead, they were grateful to have had a job and appreciative of the generosity of the employer. The silence of these workers speaks louder than the grumbling of the first-hour workers.

In the Jesus economy, grace is unfair. It is dispensed at the discretion of the Master. This truth may cause us to resent grace, because it is humbling to be unable to earn it. We desire self-sufficiency. We like to be in control, to have the last word. But grace doesn't allow us to cling to self-reliance or self-righteousness. Instead, it prompts us to cling to Christ and his work on our behalf.

The older brother in Jesus' parable of the prodigal son certainly resented his younger brother, who had done the unthinkable. But perhaps what he resented most was his father's lavish grace when welcoming his younger brother back into the home. Many times we are like the older brother, resenting those we deem as unworthy of God's grace. We look down at those who we believe know less than us, work less than us, or have less to offer than we do. If we grasp that the gap between our sinfulness and God's holiness is massive, then our sense of fairness is put into proper perspective. When we grasp that everything we have or achieve is ultimately a gift of grace, we are in a position to love our neighbors rightly. As recipients of grace, we can extend grace to others. A Godward focus continually moves us in the direction of grace.

One of the most important things to keep in mind, if we are to rebuild the ruins of broken neighborhoods and cities, is that we must embrace a posture of grace. We are the unworthy recipients of gospel grace; how can we not extend grace to others? In loving our neighbor rightly, there is no place for spiritual pride or arrogance. All that we know and all that we have is ultimately a gift of grace from our Lord. The most valuable currency of the Jesus economy is grace.

Andy Crouch reminds us of the importance of the transforming power of the gospel of grace, particularly as it relates to our call to restore justice and rebuild the ruins of our broken world.

> No image bearer can fully return to their true calling without finding themselves rescued and redeemed by the true Image Bearer, so no serious Christian witness in the world can fail to call people to put their trust in Jesus and the true God he makes known. And no image bearer can bear full witness to the glory of the Creator without the conditions for flourishing that are summed up in the rich biblical conception of justice.[5]

A GOSPEL ECOSYSTEM

A proper Godward focus is not only graciously gospel centered, it also nourishes a gospel ecosystem where multiple churches and Christian organizations with a movement mindset work together for the flourishing of a city with the integration of faith, work, and economics as a central component. Pastor Tim Keller insightfully describes a gospel ecosystem: "Just as a biological ecosystem is made of interdependent organisms, systems and natural forces, a gospel ecosystem is made of interdependent organizations, individuals, ideas, and spiritual and human forces. When all the elements of an ecosystem are in place and in balance, the entire system produces health and growth as a whole and for the elements themselves."[6] Vital to a vibrant gospel ecosystem in a community or city is the renewing and planting of gospel-centered churches. In common grace and the common cause of the common good, other institutions, such as business and government, must also be engaged in promoting the flourishing of a city.

For a gospel ecosystem to flourish in a community or city, pastors and Christian leaders must take seriously the task to equip congregants not for the minority of their lives but for the tasks they are engaged in the majority of their time. A more comprehensive discipleship approach will connect Sunday worship with Monday work, enabling congregants to live, share, and grow in their faith within their vocational callings and remunerative work.

From cradle to grave, a robust theology of faith, work, and economics will be woven into the fabric of the teaching ministries of the local church. A liturgical regularity reflecting the integration of work and economics will be evident when the local church gathers. Sermons, singing, pastoral prayers, testimonies, and benedictions will reflect a more robust theology that connects Sunday worship with the everyday life of work and the economy. Pastors and Christian leaders will seek to grow in their understanding of work and economic life, equipping the congregation for a gospel that speaks into every nook and cranny of their life in the world. Workplace visits will become as normative as hospital visits. A pastoral reading diet will not only include theology but also economics. Current economic challenges and trends will play a role in the formulation of local church strategy.

Christian leaders and pastors will find they are being more effective in the stewardship of the spiritual formation of congregations when they grasp that a great deal of spiritual growth takes place in the workplace and everyday economic life. Rick Goossen is on target when he writes, "The workplace presents most people with the greatest opportunity for spiritual growth. It is not only where we experience the soul-sapping struggles, but it is also where the fruit of God's Spirit gets unfolded within us. This critical spiritual growth does not take place only or even mainly in retreats or church services, but in the rough and tumble of enterprise."[7]

Teaching on the essential ministry of the Holy Spirit in the life of the Jesus-follower will emphasize the supernatural empowerment necessary for everyday work. If we are to walk moment by moment in the Spirit, we must recognize that we certainly will work in the Spirit. The fruit of the Spirit nourishes a flourishing ecosystem not only in the local church but also in the workplace and in society as a whole. The values and virtues of workers and economic actors within workplaces where economic exchange and wealth creation take place matter for everyone. How much more creative, innovative, enjoyable, and productive would our workplaces be if the fruit of the Spirit—love, joy, peace, patience, kindness, goodness, faithfulness, gentleness, and self-control—were regularly evident instead of deeds of the flesh? What would take place in our economy if more and more followers of Jesus were salt and light by working in and displaying the fruits of the Spirit at work? Imagine how much Spirit-empowered neighborly love would positively influence the cultures and productivity of for-profit enterprises, nonprofit enterprises, and institutions of education and government? Indeed, the church as a cultural institution plays an important role in economic flourishing.

Economists Victor Claar and Robin Klay, while affirming the importance of free markets for human flourishing, also emphasize that free markets are not sufficient for societies to thrive.

> Democracy and free markets may be counted among humanity's greatest social inventions. But the effectiveness of both these extraordinary institutions and the well-being of society depend on the presence of dynamic moral and cultural institutions as well. Such institutions provide the social glue that unites and equips people for common action based on shared values.[8]

When local churches are faithfully present in their community, empowered by the Spirit, and living out their unique expertise in spiritual formation, they are wonderfully positioned to add the vital social glue necessary for the flourishing of a diverse community.

Within a gospel ecosystem, fruitful evangelism takes place. Local church evangelism strategies must encourage congregants to live out the gospel in the workplace. Often, the gospel is seen before it is clearly heard. Common grace that loves and affirms all image bearers of God is the fertile soil where saving grace sprouts and grows. One of the apostle Paul's strongest treatises on the centrality of saving grace also includes a commitment to common grace: "So, then, as we have opportunity, let us do good to everyone, and especially to those who are of the household of faith" (Gal 6:10). Preaching and teaching pastors need to take seriously the false cultural narratives that often hinder many listeners from grasping the truthfulness and plausibility of the gospel, just as congregants need to be equipped to be wise and winsome evangelists, lovingly yet boldly proclaiming the good news to colleagues in the workplace.[9] Bill Peel speaks of this bottom-line stewardship and strategic opportunity. "God calls every Christian to be a witness for Him. So for most of us, our mission field is where we spend the bulk of our time: the workplace."[10] Bill goes on to describe the bottom line of evangelism: "Evangelism is a process, not an event. God has gifted each of us to play a critical role in drawing people to himself. Our job is to discover where the Holy Spirit is working in a person's life and join him there."[11] On both a social and individual basis, the gospel is the most powerful transformational agent imaginable, but it must be boldly shared through verbal proclamation if it is to take root and yield fruit.[12]

MOVING FORWARD

The task of rebuilding the ruins around us can only begin once we see the great need in our communities. That task is then empowered as we maintain a Godward focus, embracing the Jesus economy of grace and seeking to serve within the broader gospel ecosystem. Adopting these patterns of seeing and thinking is the initial step as we pursue cultural, spiritual, and economic renewal for the good of our neighbors, but it is not a final step. We must consider our personal productivity and the opportunities available for others to engage in meaningful work as we pursue the common good of our cities.

12

GETTING TO WORK

To live well is to work well.

THOMAS AQUINAS

In all toil there is profit,
but mere talk tends only to poverty.

PROVERBS 14:23

One of the greatest challenges confronting us when implementing a process of change is overcoming initial inertia. The weight of the way things have always been often anchors us to familiar habits and well-worn approaches. Even when an organization or leader has identified areas where change is needed, inertia can keep things from moving forward. Similarly, thoughtful leaders can be stymied by the paralysis of analysis as they consider various plans of action. There is great danger in merely discussing necessary actions without ever acting. What's needed is forward movement. As Will Rogers once said, "Even if you're on the right track, you'll get run over if you just sit there."

Rebuilding the ruins around us requires that we first embrace new patterns of seeing and thinking. But it also requires us to get to work.

In his plan to rebuild the Jerusalem wall, Nehemiah focused on getting people back to work. With the ruin and rubble of a discouraged people and a broken economy all around him, Nehemiah calls the leaders together with a big challenge and paints a hopeful picture of a better future. "Then I said to them, 'You see the trouble we are in, how Jerusalem lies in ruins with its gates burned. Come, let us build the wall of Jerusalem, that we may no longer suffer derision'" (Neh 2:17). Brick by brick, stone by stone, what had been understood as a hopeless situation begins to change as everyone gets back to work, building the wall that was destroyed. Nehemiah explains, "So we built the wall. And all the wall was joined together to half its height, for the people had a mind to work" (Neh 4:6). Against all odds and facing great opposition, the wall that had lain in ruin for decades was rebuilt in fifty-two days. What a remarkable testimony to the hard work that neighborly love requires. When people are motivated and able to work, economic flourishing often emerges.

If we are going to help rebuild the ruins of our communities and cities, an essential requirement will be for pastors and Christian leaders to cultivate a mindset to work within their congregations and the broader community. Productive work that adds value to others matters not only to God but also to our neighbors. Productivity and the profit it brings serve as the vibrant engine of a robust economy. In the long run, an economy can only continue to grow and flourish if its labor force grows in size and productivity. In a dynamically changing economy, opportunity for new job creation and the formation of new enterprises are of prime importance. The changing nature of human work itself demands exponential entrepreneurial energy and activity.

ENTREPRENEURSHIP AND JOB CREATION

One of the most reliable indicators of a vibrant economy is the number of new jobs being created. At the heart of job creation and innovation is entrepreneurship, which speaks to how people take risks to create and grow organizations. Entrepreneurs create value by solving problems in new and innovative ways in order to meet human desires, needs, and wants. Entrepreneurial enterprises and small businesses are the major engine of job creation. Management expert Peter Drucker says, "Entrepreneurship is neither a science nor an art. It is a practice."[1] Grasping the importance of entrepreneurship in both for-profit and nonprofit sectors, pastors and Christian leaders are wise to nurture a faith-driven, risk-taking environment in their congregations. This means gaining a greater understanding of the world of entrepreneurship and the qualities needed to identify and encourage entrepreneurial leaders.[2]

Pioneering churches have already taken steps toward this critical work. Real Life Assemblies of God in Midlothian, Virginia, has embraced the task of encouraging entrepreneurship. Real Life's lead pastor, Svetlana Papazov, and her team are thinking creatively about how better to connect Sunday to Monday by using the church's facilities as a business incubator. During the weekdays, Real Life hosts the Real Life Center for Entrepreneurial Innovation and Leadership Excellence. The coworking space is a busy hub for entrepreneurial innovation and development. Aspiring entrepreneurs are able to network and are encouraged as they develop skills to start or to take the next steps in building their business idea or concept.

Similarly, Oak Cliff Bible Fellowship in Dallas has bolstered their efforts to support entrepreneurs. Under the leadership of Pastor Tony Evans, Oak Cliff is working to empower new business startups through its Entrepreneurship Loyalist Program. The program features a twenty-six-week business incubation training curriculum designed to equip and encourage those who are considering starting a business. Oak Cliff has partnered with a local bank to be a primary source of business loans for new businesses birthed within their program. The church has also created a financial resource pool where entrepreneurs can get a sixty-to-ninety-day cash infusion when they are experiencing cash flow challenges. Along with training and financial assistance, the church also makes available to each aspiring entrepreneur a business mentor/consultant. As entrepreneurial endeavors gain economic traction, they are encouraged to help fund other entrepreneurs who are entering into the Entrepreneurship Loyalist Program.

My understanding of the world of entrepreneurship has been greatly expanded through the 1 Million Cups initiative launched by the Kauffman Foundation. The 1 Million Cups entrepreneurial initiative began in Kansas City in 2012 and has now spread to many cities across the United States. On Wednesday mornings, against the welcoming backdrop of great cups of coffee and the buzz of friendly conversation, one or two early startup entrepreneurs present their ideas to a diverse audience of peers, mentors, educators, and venture capitalists.[3] The conversations are electric. When I attend I not only enjoy the great coffee but also share a common passion with those who gather because we all grasp the importance of fostering entrepreneurship in our city.

George Brooks and Dan Linhart are two entrepreneurs who have helped make 1 Million Cups a great success. As members of our local church congregation, George and Dan have been catalysts for creating more of an entrepreneurial culture in our city. Together, George and Dan launched Crema (cremalab.com), a new for-profit company. Crema is a creative agency that provides business strategy, design, user experience, and technology services to new ventures and some of the world's most innovative organizations. Though Crema is not a Christian company, George and Dan's Christian faith and the neighborly love it empowers flow through the values they cherish and are on clear display in the vibrant culture they've fostered within their thriving business enterprise. At a conference sponsored by our local church, the entrepreneurship embodied in Crema was enthusiastically celebrated. What we celebrate often shouts out what we value most.

A local church that desires to embrace a neighborly love of compassion and capacity will seek to be an encouraging incubator for entrepreneurial thinking and entrepreneurs in both the profit and nonprofit sectors. As a licensed professional counselor, Kori Bohn had a dream of starting a clinic that would better serve those with eating disorders. With the assistance of several members of our congregation, including a lawyer who drew up incorporation papers and a pastor who worked on marketing strategy, Renew Counseling Center opened its doors in Kansas City. Today, it continues to meet the needs of a struggling population in our city.[4] A local church committed to rebuilding the ruins of a city nurtures an organizational culture where entrepreneurship and job creation are valued and celebrated.

JOBS AND POVERTY

If we care for the poor, we must care for business. Entrepreneur Magatte Wade passionately and persuasively argues if people really cared about helping the poor and addressing poverty, they would focus on business. Magatte puts it bluntly, "The most powerful poverty alleviation tool is a job."[5] As pastors and Christian leaders we must take job creation seriously and leverage our roles to foster conditions conducive for flourishing economies. Chris Horst and Peter Greer get right to the point. "Jobs are the central weapon in the war on poverty. They are the centerpiece of communities that flourish."[6] While nonprofit organizations play an important role in poverty alleviation, for-profit enterprises are essential. Horst and Greer conclude, "After looking at the data about what transforms poverty stricken communities in a lasting way, we have come to the conclusion that if you care about the poor, you simply must care about business and entrepreneurship. Nonprofit organizations play important roles in flourishing societies, but they work only if they are supplementing a vibrant business community."[7] Robert Lupton also weighs in on the centrality of jobs and the importance of the church pursuing job creation for many who are marginalized and vulnerable in society. "The only thing that moves a person out of poverty is a job. That's it. So the next question we need to ask is, 'Are we facilitating the creation of jobs that enable people to move out of poverty?' The answer is no, we're not."[8]

While an increasing number of pastors are teaching members of congregations that their work matters, all too few share the same commitment to highlighting the importance of job creation in their communities and cities. It is not just that work matters, having a job also matters. Heralding the goodness of Christian compassion is one thing; working toward wealth creation and expanding economic capacity in a community is another. When it comes to poverty alleviation, neighborly love fueled by compassion without concern for capacity will ultimately prove ineffective and frustrating. For-profit business enterprises are essential for the flourishing of all people of a community, particularly the most vulnerable.

PERSONAL PRODUCTIVITY GROWTH

Not only is getting a job important, so too is growing in job skill and personal productivity. Increasing personal productivity enables us to find greater job satisfaction as well as add greater value to the economy, enhancing the common good. The more skilled and productive we become, the more likely our economic capacity will grow, which means our opportunity to enact compassion-fueled neighborly love will also increase.

It is encouraging that many local churches have promoted programs advocating wiser money management and better financial fitness for their congregants.[9] What is not encouraging is how few churches have dedicated time and effort toward initiatives designed to help congregants expand their economic capacity through greater personal productivity. No matter what our work context is, personal productivity is not just about working harder but working wiser. Becoming a more productive person in our work is much more about increasing our effectiveness than merely ramping up the speed of our activity. Productivity is not merely doing things right, but first and foremost doing the right things for the right reasons.

As apprentices of Jesus, our motivation for greater productivity is not personal pride or materialistic indulgence, but rather sincere desire to increase our God-honoring stewardship and our capacity for neighborly love. Matt Perman provides choice nuggets of practical wisdom regarding personal productivity growth. Matt embraces a gospel centricity asserting the close linkage between a life of discipleship and a life of productivity. Thinking Christianly about personal productivity, Matt writes, "There is no distinction between learning how to be productive and learning how to live the Christian life altogether, for both are about how we are to live in this world for the glory of God."[10] Encouraging not only a strong work ethic but also personal work productivity is an important component of discipleship into greater Christlikeness. As a small business owner, Jesus the carpenter from Nazareth would applaud efforts to increase work productivity.

A practical step forward for a local church is to provide seminars and classes that equip congregants in personal and productivity management skills.[11] It is not just that work matters, how we do our work matters too. A fruitful and productive life is a telling mark of a faithful life. If we are going to rebuild the ruins of a crumbling culture, job creation and productivity growth matter. We must get to work. We also must pursue the common good.

PURSUING THE COMMON GOOD

Nehemiah risked his own life, invested his own resources, and worked tirelessly for the common good of his city. He took the lead in ensuring that the Jerusalem wall was built for all the people by all the people. Everyone pitched in for the good of everyone.

Nehemiah also took the lead in confronting the systemic economic injustice of his day. He stood against exploitation of the poor, whose land was being mortgaged away and whose children were being enslaved during a time of famine. Nehemiah also confronted the practice of heaping excessive interest on the backs of the poor. Nehemiah doesn't dance around the egregious injustice: "So I said, 'The thing that you are doing is not good. Ought you not to walk in the fear of our God to prevent the taunts of the nations of our enemies?'" (Neh 5:9).

A serious commitment to pursuing the common good expresses itself in tireless work toward helping the most vulnerable members of a community flourish. A comprehensive and collaborative approach is required. Efforts should include addressing education issues in underresourced communities and working with graduates of underperforming schools, who often are unprepared for the academic rigors of college and lack the basic job skills needed for entering the work force.[12] Inadequate access to health care, substandard housing, and neighborhood safety must also be addressed in any plan for meaningful long-term engagement. Brian Fikkert and Steve Corbett suggest three distinct yet interconnected categories for addressing poverty alleviation and fostering the common good. First, *relief* responds to crisis, addressing immediate, urgent human needs. Second, *rehabilitation* follows on the heels of crisis, focusing on restoring individuals and communities to pre-crisis status. And third, *development* is a long-term, comprehensive strategy and empowering process that seeks to cultivate greater community flourishing.[13]

The local church I serve has used this threefold framing of relief, rehabilitation, and development as a guiding framework for our missional investment in poverty alleviation. We have also sought to build into our missional strategy five antipoverty building blocks. First, we are committed to planting churches and nurturing local church health that promotes a flourishing gospel ecosystem. Second, we work with both the private and public sectors to provide a safety net for the most vulnerable in our city. Third, we are committed to serve in the area of education, particularly in low-performing schools. Our congregation is involved in many ways, including tutoring, assisting in parenting skills, after-school programs, and providing job opportunities. We are also involved and invested in the broader arts community.[14] Fourth, we take a long-term approach, collaborating with a wide variety of individuals and institutions with the goal of comprehensive neighborhood rebuilding. Fifth, we are increasingly looking for ways to partner with business in stimulating economic growth through job creation.

When it comes to poverty alleviation and the common good, Fikkert and Corbett offer a helpful perspective: "In summary, poor people in North America could benefit from all of the following: (1) the ability to work at jobs with living wages, (2) the capacity to manage their money, (3) the opportunity to accumulate wealth, and (4) a greater supply of quality education, housing, and health care at affordable rates."[15]

Nehemiah not only rebuilt a wall, he was committed to restoring a people and renewing a community spiritually.[16] For a community to truly flourish, it needs spiritual resources and empowerment. When we pursue the common good, a top priority must be the planting and renewal of local churches that proclaim the gospel and are committed to the spiritual formation of individuals and families.

VOCATIONAL STEWARDSHIP

If we are serious about pursuing the common good, we will see that a primary work of the church is the church at work.[17] Local churches can have a profound influence in their communities through the myriad of for-profit and nonprofit workplaces congregation members occupy during the week. When a local church embraces more robust vocational missiology, there will be a greater emphasis on equipping congregants for greater vocational stewardship. Amy Sherman speaks with remarkable insight regarding the importance of vocational stewardship, which she defines as "the intentional and strategic deployment of our vocational power—knowledge, platform, networks, position, influence, skills, and reputation—to advance God's kingdom."[18] Every local church has a vast potential for promoting the common good in and through each congregant's vocational calling. The local church often talks about stewarding financial resources well, but it all too seldom helps congregants see the vast influence they might have by stewarding their vocational power effectively.

Sherman suggests four helpful pathways for deploying congregants in the stewardship of their vocations: (1) blooming where congregants are planted by strategically stewarding our current job, (2) donating vocational skills as a volunteer, (3) launching a social enterprise, and (4) participating in a targeted congregational initiative aimed at transforming a particular community or solving a specific social problem.[19]

In addition to equipping congregants for their individual vocational stewardship, Christian leaders and pastors committed to the common good will seek to maximize the synergy of overlapping networks, forging collaborative partnerships. Nehemiah didn't approach the massive task of rebuilding Jerusalem's wall thinking he could do it alone. Neither can we. With humility of heart, a spirit of teachability, and hopeful realism, we need to join hands in mutual collaboration for the common good and the glory of God.

THE GOODNESS OF COLLABORATIVE PARTNERSHIPS

The predominately suburban church I serve has been enriched for nearly two decades by joining hearts and hands with an urban church we partner with to bring shalom to our city. Christian Fellowship Baptist Church, led by Pastor Stan Archie, is a bright light of hope in our city. As two churches committed to the gospel, to one another, and to our city, we have enjoyed the rich fellowship and joyful satisfaction of being a beacon of hopeful reconciliation and resurrection unity to our wounded city. Over the years we have exchanged pulpits, built homes together, focused on educational initiatives, hosted joint conferences, planned youth, women's, and leadership retreats, and rolled up our sleeves in countless ways for the glory of Christ and the common good of our city.

Both churches bring unique strengths and resources to the table of our collaborative partnership. We truly are better together both in the beauty of our expression and the effectiveness of our mission. Together we have worked to be quiet catalysts in bringing together more urban and suburban churches who are committed to pursuing the common good of our city. One of the more hopeful signs in our wounded metropolitan area is the growing number of predominately white suburban churches entering into friendships and partnerships with predominately African American and Hispanic urban churches.

While true collaborative partnerships are still far too rare, I am encouraged that more churches are working together to rebuild the cities where they have been sovereignly planted to be salt and light. The challenging times we live in and the ruins we are encountering call for pastors and Christian leaders who are faithfully present in the culture, firmly centered in the gospel, and humbly willing to see themselves implicated in the brokenness of our world.

Theologian Richard Hays encourages the church to shift its primary focus from the aim of reforming society to that of experiencing the power of the resurrection in our midst.[20] One telling sign of resurrection power in any local congregation is that Sunday worship is understood as being closely connected to Monday work and the economy. Resurrection power is evidenced in a faith community when increasing neighborly love of both compassion and capacity is deployed for the proclamation of the gospel and the furtherance of the common good—all for the glory of God. Church historian Charlie Self keeps the big picture in mind when he observes, "the aim of our integration of faith, work, and economics is not conservatism or liberalism. The aim is the glory of God and the flourishing *of* our communities."[21]

13

THE HOPE OF THE WORLD

Faith and pessimism are incompatible.
To be sure, we are not starry-eyed idealists;
we are down to earth realists. We know well that sin
is ingrained in human nature and in human society. We are not
expecting to build a utopia. But we also know that the gospel has
transforming power and that Christ has commissioned us
to be effective salt and light in the world. So let us
offer ourselves to God as agents of change.

JOHN STOTT

I will build my church, and the gates
of hell will not prevail against it

MATTHEW 16:18

After attending a conference in New York City, a pastoral colleague, Reid Kapple, was flying home to Kansas City on US Airways flight 745 when the plane suddenly lost cabin pressure. As the plane descended quickly, the oxygen masks deployed from above. A sense of fear filled the plane. Reid wondered if he would see his family again. When the plane reached ten thousand feet, the captain informed the passengers that everything was operational and that they would be landing soon. Breathing a bit easier, Reid looked more closely at the oxygen mask he held in his hand. He noticed it was manufactured by B/E Aerospace in Lenexa, Kansas, a Kansas City suburb near his family's home.

Later, as Reid was preparing a sermon on the ways that work plays a vital role in loving our neighbors, he thought about the workers at B/E Aerospace who had made the oxygen masks that allowed him to breathe in a plane with lost cabin pressure. He quickly crafted an email describing what had happened on flight 745, thanking B/E Aerospace for their contribution to his safe return to Kansas City. Pastor Reid concluded his email with these words:

> If I may be so bold, I would like to thank God for the work he has called and equipped your company to do. I know that not many people think of work like this as being work God cares about, but I strongly beg to differ. I believe that God cares deeply about all work that is done well and promotes human flourishing. So again, thank you for your work. Please, by all means, keep doing what you are doing and do it well for the common good of all. Thankfully, Reid Kapple

Much to Reid's surprise, the vice president of B/E Aerospace, J. P. Foulon, quickly responded. He thanked Reid, a pastor he had never met, for his affirming words and invited him to come and share his story with all the employees of the company. Reid enthusiastically accepted the gracious invitation. A few weeks later, Pastor Reid spoke to the entire company, sharing his story and expressing his gratitude for each person's work. He told the employees of B/E Aerospace that the work they do, no matter how mindless or meaningless it may feel, matters to God because it matters to their neighbors. After Reid's presentation, many employees came up to him afterwards, and with tears in their eyes expressed how much his words meant to them, affirming that Reid's message had instilled within them a renewed vision, imagination, and joy in their work.

The life Pastor Reid lives, the message he communicates, and the local church he serves all speak to the vital importance of connecting Sunday worship with Monday work and the economy. In a time when the local church is often marginalized, opportunities for neighborly love, gospel impact, and positive cultural influence are brimming with possibilities—if we are willing to engage the world of work. Yet it will take Spirit-empowered pastors and church leaders who out of theological conviction embrace a more robust missional paradigm that takes seriously the stewardship of equipping congregations for a majority of their lives. At the heart of local church mission is the intentional multiplication of Jesus' apprentices who embody neighborly love in the workplace, adding value in the broader economy. A primary work of the church is the church at work.

Pastors and Christian leaders must grasp the centrality of the local church in promoting neighborly love of compassion and capacity that pursues the common good and advances the mission of God in the world. It is all too easy to point out the flaws of the local church or even to see it as an encumbrance to advancing the work of God in the world. Despite the local church's frailties, shortcomings, and failures, the local church as God designed it is the hope of the world. Christ has not given up on his church. We must not either.

John Stott gets to the heart of the matter:

For the church lies at the very center of the eternal purposes of God. It is not a divine afterthought. It is not an accident of history. On the contrary, the church is God's new community. For his purpose, conceived in past eternity, being worked out in history, and to be perfected in a future eternity, is not just to save isolated individuals and so perpetuate our loneliness, but rather to build his church, that is, to call out of the world a people for his own glory.[1]

In the midst of endless emails, pastoral care issues, budget meetings, and local church leadership challenges, it is easy for the "big why" of the church to get fuzzy. Indeed, it is always easy for the "big why" of what we do to get lost in the unending details of how we do what we do. Simon Sinek writes, "By WHY I mean what is your purpose, cause or belief? WHY does your company exist? WHY do you get out of bed every morning? And WHY should anyone care?"[2] It is not what we do or how we do it that matters most. It's why we do what we do that makes all the difference. Having clarity in the "big why" of our local church mission is crucial.

BEYOND COMPASSION

As God's new creation community, the local church must not merely embody compassion for the world but also play a vital role in building capacity for the world. This means we must bring our Christian faith, our work, and our economics together with a wise and integral approach, like the good Samaritan, who exhibited both compassion and capacity. If we focus on capacity building without nurturing compassion, we may well become patronizing and insensitive to the complex challenges faced by our underresourced neighbors. If we have compassion without capacity, we may well become judgmental and strident toward those who seem not to care as we do about the economic realities of others. Individuals and organizations that don't take seriously the importance of capacity building face both the challenge of fruitlessness and frustration.

The New Testament writer James speaks to the importance of the church and economic realities. James calls the church to deeds of faith that exhibit more than mere compassion. "If a brother or sister is poorly clothed and lacking in daily food, and one of you says to them, 'Go in peace, be warmed and filled,' without giving them the things needed for the body, what good is that?" (Jas 2:15-16). Underlying James's godly admonition to rightful compassion is the economic capacity to actually love others in a dignity-affirming and God-honoring way. Without building economic capacity through wealth creation, the modern church is saying to its fellow citizens in need, "Go in peace, be unemployed and underemployed, and be dependent on government." But if we bring both greater compassion and increased capacity to the world, the local church will once again exemplify a true neighborly love and advance our gospel mission.

BRINGING FAITH, WORK, AND ECONOMICS TOGETHER

I believe the wind of the Spirit is blowing across our nation and the globe, stirring up churches and church leaders to strategically address the Sunday-to-Monday gap, to more passionately and intentionally bring faith, work, and economics together in a seamless fabric of missional faithfulness and fruitfulness. In a time when the Christian church is increasingly perceived as adding little value to a community, doors for local church gospel mission are opening wide as a result of faithful and thoughtful church engagement of work and economics.

In his book *The Coming Jobs War*, Jim Clifton, chairman and CEO of the Gallup Association, summarizes conclusions from data gathered by surveying over 120,000 people in 150 countries of the world. Clifton writes, "Six years into our global collection effort, we may have already found the single most searing, clarifying, helpful, world-altering fact. What the whole world wants is a good job."[3] What will the church's response be to this cry in this moment in history?

While the world is crying out for jobs and for greater economic opportunity, churches are beginning to respond in very encouraging ways. Local church leaders are building into their strategic planning not only growing evangelism, attendance, and small group discipleship goals but also job creation and wealth creation targets.

All too often businesspeople in the church are seen primarily as candidates for serving on the building or finance committees. While these are good places to serve, what if these gifted servants of God were released to put more of their energy into what they do best—creating jobs and building economic capacity in our local and global economies? What if, as a part of our local church strategies, we would seek to stoke the fires of entrepreneurship and set targets for a specific number of good jobs created each year? I would like to see us celebrate not only the missionaries we send around the globe but also the jobs we create around the world. Let's celebrate with the same enthusiasm the formation of new for-profit businesses as we do the formation of new nonprofit organizations. What if the church we have been called to serve would invest more resources in creating sustainable, tax-generating, charity-donating jobs? How would this initiative ignite the imagination and passions of the business domain within the church?

Local churches and church leaders are not only seeking ways to build capacity, they are also increasingly mapping out their present capacity to extend neighborly love to their communities. It is crucial to see the local church not only as a dynamic organism but also as a stable, well-managed institution that maintains a faithful presence in a community over the long haul.

No matter the size of the local church, it is a vital economic actor within a community. The local church often has a sizeable real estate footprint, multiple buildings, and a sizeable asset balance sheet. In many cases a growing local church is a job creator and significant employer that has the opportunity to create environments where employees flourish. The local church can set the bar for leadership and management excellence, both in the profit and nonprofit sectors.

What does a more intentional faith, work, and economics focus look like in a local church? The answer is as varied as the theological contours of the congregation as well as the contexts God has sovereignly placed each local church to serve in.

An increasing number of churches are thinking creatively and strategically about how better to embrace a neighborly love of compassion and capacity. High Point Church of Christ in Princeton, Texas, offers seed capital for new businesses launched by church members. Olivet Baptist Church, in Chattanooga, underwrites college scholarships for underresourced youth who will be the first in their families to seek a college education. Tabernacle Community Church in Grand Rapids sponsors the Youth Entrepreneur Leadership Program. In this program middle school students are exposed to entrepreneurship teaching for seven weeks during the summer. Students develop business plans and present them to local entrepreneurs in a "Shark Tank" environment. City Hope Church in Akron, Ohio, is a new startup church, committed to strong faith, work, and economic integration. As a young church plant, City Hope Church has launched an open-choice food pantry. As the description implies, people have choice in the groceries they select at the food pantry. Those who shop and those who help the shoppers share a meal together.

ADDRESSING THE SUNDAY-TO-MONDAY GAP

When it comes to faith, work, and economic integration, how are you and your church doing? Are you thoughtfully addressing the Sunday-to-Monday gap? I am hopeful that in reading these chapters you not only have some new questions to consider, but you also have gained some important information that can lead you to thoughtful action. Neighborly love is more than sentimental compassion; it is also a call toward active capacity building. Steven Garber reminds us that knowing and responsibility go hand in hand. What we know implicates us in what we do or don't do. Steve writes, "In every century and every culture there is an integral connection between knowing and doing, and it is most fully expressed in love. For glory or shame, we choose to live in love—or not."[4]

Perhaps it is time to carve out some time for fervent prayer and honest assessment, both on an individual as well as an institutional level. Some personal time away for reflection as well as leadership team retreats are great places for this kind of work to begin. Where are the gaps that need to be addressed in your preaching, teaching, liturgy, discipleship, and overall church mission? Are members of your congregation increasingly informed in breadth and depth about what the Scriptures say about work and economics? How are you seeing the local church as a vital economic actor in your community and city? My prayer is that thoughtful reflection might lead you toward a congregational mission that more seriously embraces neighborly love which nurtures Christlike compassion as well as economic capacity within the life of your local church.

Against the painful backdrop of my impoverished youth, as well as my thirty years of experience as a local church pastor, I believe human flourishing and economic flourishing are intricately connected and inextricably linked. What a difference the local church of my childhood would have made in the flourishing of our family had it taken seriously the gospel's comprehensive outworking in all dimensions of human existence. How profoundly transforming it would have been had my faith community encouraged and celebrated the nurturing of economic capacity and wealth creation in the same way it celebrated personal piety and sacrificial acts of Christian compassion.

I realize that for many pastors and Christian leaders economics can seem overwhelmingly complex, riddled with a myriad of ideological minefields, and peripheral to the local church's mission in the world. While these perceived obstacles may still be somewhat daunting to us, they must not prevent us from taking seriously the profound stewardship of nurturing both Christian compassion and economic capacity. In a time when the local church is often marginalized and even despised by some, a wide window of missional opportunity is opening to the church. Will we embrace this opportunity to address the cries of our communities, our cities, and our world for jobs sweet jobs? Will we hit our knees and roll up our sleeves and with renewed Spirit passion affirm human dignity and promote greater economic flourishing?

Like no other institution in society, the local church is uniquely designed to be a catalyst of human flourishing. In almost every rural, suburban, and urban community the local church is already present and strategically positioned to bring deep and lasting transformation to individuals, families, and social structures. While many social observers and pundits are lamenting the moral decline of culture, the local church can be a hopeful catalyst for spiritual and moral awakening. Resting in the sovereignty of God and trusting in his perfect will, I pray to this end.

Imagine how God would be glorified, the gospel would be embraced, and our communities would flourish if pastors and Christian leaders in the power of the Holy Spirit embraced a concentrated and sustained effort to narrow the Sunday-to-Monday gap. Local congregations with growing economic capacity would unleash greater and wiser generosity as well as increasingly be perceived in the community as adding value to society. Generous and collaborative common-good initiatives aimed at the most vulnerable members of society would become increasingly common. Local churches would encourage through their membership entrepreneurial risk taking and celebrate job creation. With technological innovation being indispensable for increasing standards of living, local churches would play a vital role, not only encouraging emerging technologies but also providing needed moral reflection on those technologies.

Many pastors and Christian leaders are awakening to a moment of great gospel opportunity. What changes in our local church do we need to embrace? What unique opportunities in our communities are waiting to be engaged with renewed passion and commitment? For the glory of God and the flourishing of our neighbors, let's seize the moment.

ACKNOWLEDGMENTS

I n a garden long ago, Adam was not only given a job to do, he was also given someone to work with—his remarkable soulmate, Eve. In the grace gift of my bride, Liz, daily I see glimpses of the beauty and goodness of God's masterful design. Thank you, Liz, for your unwavering devotion to Christ and to our marriage, and for the generous fruitfulness of your extraordinary life. Thanks for sacrificing an entire summer so that this project could become a reality.

At the end of the day, every good endeavor is truly a collaborative work. My pastoral colleague Tyler Chernesky provided constant encouragement and tireless assistance in reworking the manuscript. Tyler's tender heart, contagious joy, and brilliant mind are a rare treasure. My colleague Marcia Petersen not only assisted with the manuscript but also joyfully covered a myriad of details. Marcia has the unique ability to skate where the puck is going to be. Thanks, Marcia.

Greg Forster, PJ Hill, Scott Rae, and Josh Good read the manuscript and offered invaluable assistance along the way. My Made to Flourish colleagues have provided so much encouragement in seeing this project through to completion. Thank you Matt Rusten, Luke Bobo, Melissa Emerson, Charlie Self, Matt Perman, Tara Bowers, Marcia Petersen, and Dave Huber.

An unexpected joy for me has been serving with the Oikonomia Network. Greg Forster, Scott Rae, Chris Armstrong, Gerry Breshears, Donald Guthrie, PJ Hill, and Charlie Self have not only become conversational partners but dear friends. A warm word of thanks is also due to Os Guinness, James Hunter, Brian Fikkert, Andy Crouch, Tim Keller, David Dockery, Don Carson, Rick Lints, David Gill, Bill Peel, Mark Roberts, Darrell Bock, Mark McCloskey, Mike Metzger, Skye Jethani, and Katherine Leary Alsdorf, whose encouraging input into my life and work is greatly appreciated. I also want to thank the late Dallas Willard, whose friendship, writings, and imprint on my life are beyond measure.

I am deeply grateful for the Christ Community Church family that I have the privilege of serving. You truly are a congregation that loves as Jesus loves—with head, heart, and hands. I want to thank the Christ Community elder leadership team and staff, especially Kevin Harlan, Mark Askins, Andrew Jones, Nathan Miller, Bill Gorman, Gabe Coyle, and Tim Spanburg, who lead with integrity of heart and skillful hands. Thanks for constantly sharpening me in so many ways, particularly for helping me think how to be more faithful in connecting Sunday worship with Monday work and the economy. To pastor Stan Archie and the entire Christian Fellowship Baptist Church family, I want to say thanks for your cherished friendship and partnership in the gospel work we do together in Kansas City.

The highly capable staff of the Kern Family Foundation has been ever affirming and encouraging. A special thanks to Jim Rahn, Kyle Bode, Josh Good, Fred Oaks, and Betsy Mackett. I am thankful not only for your partnership in mission but also for your warm and endearing friendship. Keep up the good work you are doing.

I want to thank Steve Steddom for his helpful thoughts on generosity. Steve, your friendship over the years has been a gift, and your insight on philanthropy is extraordinary. I also want to thank Bethany Jenkins for her warm friendship and for encouraging our publishing partnership with InterVarsity Press. A word of thanks is also in order to Jeff Crosby and Cindy Bunch, as well as the InterVarsity Press staff, for your unwavering commitment and excellent work ethic.

There are so many sharpening friends whose endorsements and wise insights find their way both explicitly and implicitly into this book. I couldn't begin to list them all. You know who you are and I am very grateful for each of you. I especially want to express my heartfelt devotion and gratitude for my friend Steve Garber and his bride, Meg. Your devoted friendship and constant encouragement are deeply cherished. I also want to thank Amy Sherman, who continues to be not only a grace gift but also a conversational partner with never-ending insight and boundless enthusiasm.

As a pastor who knows the joys and heartaches of parish ministry, I want to offer a word of encouragement and appreciation to every pastor. Let's keep the gospel central, stay yoked to Jesus, love our neighbor, and rejoice each day in the true hope we have to offer a hopeless world.

Soli Deo Gloria

NOTES

1 NEIGHBORLY LOVE

[1]Derek Thompson, "A World Without Work," *Atlantic*, July-August 2015, 53.

[2]Joel Mokyr, "Technology and the Future of Work" (lecture, Northwestern University, December 2, 2015), www.youtube.com/watch?v=UgHbZhNiluc. Also see Joel Mokyr, Chris Vickers, and Nicolas L. Ziebarth, "The History of Technological Anxiety and the Future of Economic Growth: Is This Time Different?," *Journal of Economic Perspectives* 29, no. 3 (2015): 31-50.

[3]Klaus Issler, "Examining Jesus' Inclusion of Work Roles in His Parables," Institute for Faith, Work & Economics, accessed February 10, 2017, http://tifwe.org/wp-content/uploads/2014/04/Jesus-and-the-Parables1.pdf, 4.

[4]For an expanded discussion regarding Jesus spending the majority of his time on earth as a carpenter, see Tom Nelson, *Work Matters: Connecting Sunday Worship to Monday Work* (Wheaton, IL: Crossway, 2011), 87-88.

[5]Luke employs the Greek word *splagchnon* only three times in his Gospel (Lk 7:13; 10:33; 15:20). Each time *splagchnon* is used, it is in the context of deep feelings of pity or sympathy evoked by the dire economic need of another person. The apostle John also uses this word in 1 John 3:17, striking a negative note as he describes the absence of brotherly love within one who sees a brother in economic need and yet "closes his heart against him."

[6]Kenneth Bailey, *Jesus Through Middle Eastern Eyes: Cultural Studies in the Gospels* (Downers Grove, IL: IVP Academic, 2008), 290.

[7]Thomas Sowell, *Basic Economics: A Citizen's Guide to the Economy* (New York: Basic Books, 2001), 213.

[8]Martin Luther, quoted in Gustav Wingren, *Luther on Vocation*, trans. Carl C. Rasmussen (Evansville, IN: Ballast, 1994), 10.

[9]Dallas Willard and Gary Black Jr., *The Divine Conspiracy Continued* (San Francisco: HarperOne, 2014), 197.

[10]Robert Lupton, *Toxic Charity: How Churches and Charities Hurt Those They Help and How to Reverse It* (New York: HarperOne, 2011), 31.

[11]Personal email communication with the author, September 16, 2015.

[12]Bailey, *Jesus Through Middle Eastern Eyes*, 295.

2 MADE TO FLOURISH

[1]John F. Kilner, *Dignity and Destiny: Humanity in the Image of God* (Grand Rapids: Eerdmans, 2015), 114.

[2]Makoto Fujimura, *Culture Care: Reconnecting with Beauty for Our Common Life* (Downers Grove, IL: InterVarsity Press, 2017), 27, 100.

[3]The Hebrew word for fruitfulness is *pārah*. *Pārah* appears throughout the creation account, most notably in Genesis 1:22, 28. It also appears after the great flood, as God reissues the cultural mandate to Noah and his family in Genesis 9:1, 7. Notably, *pārâ* speaks of the products of human labor in Exodus 23:16-17.

Pārâ language is also associated with the Old Testament concept of "first fruits," which referred to offerings and tithes relating to the wealth produced from work. Proverbs 31 uses *pārâ* to speak of the productivity of the diligent, honorable woman. Indeed, Proverbs 31:16, 31 speak affirmingly of the woman's economic activity, praising "the fruit of her hands." In the New Testament, *karpos* language denotes fruitfulness, and often speaks of the result, outcome, or product of a particular course of action. For example, Matthew 7:20 states "you will recognize them by their fruits." There, the author speaks of good fruit as the product of character and good deeds. Paul uses *karpos* language in Philippians 1:22 to express that his continued earthly existence requires his continued embrace of "fruitful labor."

[4]Katelyn Beaty, *A Woman's Place: A Christian Vision for Your Calling in the Office, the Home and the World* (New York: Howard Books, 2016), 7.

[5]For a more expansive discussion of the reality that we were created to work, see Tom Nelson, *Work Matters: Connecting Sunday Worship to Monday Work* (Wheaton, IL: Crossway, 2011), 20-31.

[6]Greg Forster, *Joy to the World: How Christianity Lost Its Cultural Influence and Can Begin Rebuilding It* (Wheaton, IL: Crossway, 2014), 225.

[7]Victor V. Claar and Robin J. Klay, *Economics in Christian Perspective: Theory, Policy and Life Choices* (Downers Grove, IL: IVP Academic, 2007), 166.

3 HUMAN FRUITFULNESS AND MATERIAL WEALTH

[1]Andy Crouch, "From 'It Was Good' to 'The Glory and Honor of the Nations': The Story of Culture" (lecture, Common Good 2013, Kansas City, April 5, 2013).

[2]Peter Brown, *Through the Eye of a Needle: Wealth, the Fall of Rome, and the Making of Christianity in the West, 350-550 AD* (Princeton, NJ: Princeton

University Press, 2012), 523. For a greater understanding of how the church has wrestled with wealth and money, I highly recommend Peter Brown's brilliant treatise *Through the Eye of a Needle*. Brown is the most prestigious early church scholar in this area. He traces two divergent Christian traditions on wealth, recounting the struggle between Pelagian and Augustinian views. While Pelagian views saw renunciation of wealth as intrinsic to discipleship, Augustinian views presented the stewardship of wealth as intrinsic to discipleship. Augustine held that pride was the great enemy of Christian discipleship, not wealth. Indeed, Augustine declared, "Get rid of pride, and riches will do no harm." Peter Brown makes this point, "In Augustine's preaching, pride, not wealth was the true last enemy of the Christian. The real division of the world was not between the rich and the poor. It was between the proud and those who were enabled by God's grace to be humble before God and before their fellows. In practice this meant a view of society where the inequalities created by wealth could be accepted as long as they were softened by the abandonment of the toxic by-products of wealth—arrogance, violence, and the abuse of power" (ibid., 349).

[3] Dallas Willard, *The Spirit of the Disciplines: Understanding How God Changes Lives* (San Francisco: Harper & Row, 1998), 194. I recommend the entire chapter titled "Is Poverty Spiritual?"

[4] See Joel Osteen, *Your Best Life Now: 7 Steps to Living at Your Full Potential* (New York: Warner Books, 2004). In his bestselling book, Osteen writes, "You were born to win; you were born for greatness, you were created to be a champion in life" (p. 35). He clarifies, "God is a good God, and He gives good things to his children. No matter who has denigrated you or how much pain you've experienced in life, no matter how many setbacks you have suffered, you cannot allow yourself to accept that as the way life is supposed to be. No, God has better things in store for you. You must reprogram your mind with God's word; change that negative, defeated self-image, and start seeing yourself as winning, coming out on top. Start seeing that marriage as restored. See your business as flourishing. See your children as enjoying the good things of God. You must see it through your eyes of faith, and then it will begin to happen" (p. 63).

[5] John R. Schneider, *The Good of Affluence: Seeking God in a Culture of Wealth* (Grand Rapids: Eerdmans, 2002), 5.

[6] See Scott Rae's excellent treatment of the implications of the vast differences in economic life between a zero-sum biblical economy and today's modern

economy. Scott Rae, *Business for the Common Good* (Downers Grove, IL: IVP Academic, 2011), chap. 4.

[7]God's abundant creation design has been thwarted throughout the broad sweep of human history. Instead of wealth growing exponentially, wealth was traded, stolen, plundered, or lost. No doubt this perpetuated a fixed-pie understanding of economics. Economic growth occurs exponentially when certain legal and moral frameworks are in place. If property rights are insecure and contracts are not enforced, many times properly earned wealth is taken rather than created. In these situations, as Peter Brown astutely observes, excesses in the few leads to the dispossession of the many.

[8]Thomas Sowell, *Basic Economics: A Common Sense Guide to the Economy* (New York: Basic Books, 2000), 540.

[9]Brown, *Through the Eye of a Needle*, 315.

[10]See Tim Goodwin, "The Battle Is for the Customer Interface," *Techcrunch .com*, March 3, 2015, https//:techcrunch.com/2015/03/03/in-the-age-of -disintermediation-the-battle-is-all-for-the-customer-interface.

[11]See Angus Maddison, *Contours of the World Economy: 1-2030 AD* (Oxford: Oxford University Press, 2007).

[12]Deirdre N. McCloskey, *Bourgeois Dignity: Why Economics Can't Explain the Modern World* (Chicago: University of Chicago Press, 2010), 2.

[13]See Deirdre N. McCloskey, *Bourgeois Equality: How Ideas, Not Capital or Institutions, Enriched the World* (Chicago: University of Chicago Press, 2016). McCloskey points out the stunning rise of economic activity, wealth creation, and human betterment, making this point: "The Great Enrichment of the past two centuries has dwarfed any of the previous and temporary enrichments. Explaining it is the central scientific task of economics and economic history, and it matters for any other sort of social science or recent history" (p. xiv).

[14]See Hans Rosling, "200 Countries, 200 Years, 4 Minutes: The Joy of Stats," BBCFour, November 2010, www.youtube.com/watch?v=jbkSRLYSojo.

[15]McCloskey, *Bourgeois Equality*, 112. McCloskey asserts, "The original and sustaining causes of the modern world, in other words, were ethical and not material. They were the widening adoption of two mere ideas, the new and liberal economic idea of liberty for ordinary people and the new and democratic social idea of dignity for them" (p. xxxi).

[16]Michael Novak, *The Spirit of Democratic Capitalism: Thirty Years Later* (McLean, VA: Institute for Faith, Work & Economics, 2015), 10-11.

[17]Hernando de Soto, *The Mystery of Capital: Why Capitalism Triumphs in the West and Fails Everywhere Else* (New York: Basic Books, 2000), 102.

[18]See McCloskey, *Bourgeois Dignity*, 2.

[19]Frederick Buechner, *Wishful Thinking: A Theological ABC* (New York: Harper & Row, 1973), 118-19.

4 THE FRUITFULNESS OF FAITHFULNESS

[1]Jesus' teaching often has a reoccurring pattern of invitation, metaphor, and paradox. In Matthew 11:28-30, Jesus invites all who would be his disciples to take his yoke, learn from him, and find rest. At the heart of this invitation is the metaphor of the yoke. This metaphor normally conjures a negative connotation, suggesting human bondage and servitude. Yet here Jesus embeds a paradox within the metaphor. Jesus' yoke is paradoxical, for it is not the path to human impoverishment but rather the path to true human flourishing.

Jesus follows this same pattern of invitation, metaphor, and paradox in Matthew 16:24-25. Jesus invites all who would follow him to take up their cross. The cross, as it is evoked here by Jesus, is used metaphorically to reference death. However, embedded in the cross metaphor is a paradox of death to life. Jesus demonstrates that those who take up his cross and follow him will actually find true life. In losing our life, we find it.

In John 15, Jesus also employs the pattern of invitation, metaphor, and paradox. The invitation to abide in Jesus points to the metaphor of the grapevine. The paradox embedded in the vine metaphor is that pruning or the cutting back of fruit actually produces more fruit.

[2]From the burning bush at Horeb, Moses hears these words of promise from YHWH: "I promise that I will bring you up out of the affliction of Egypt to the land of the Canaanites, . . . a land flowing with milk and honey" (Ex 3:17).

[3]Walter F. Bauer, Wilbur Gingrich, and Frederick W. Danker note that John's use of the Greek word *menō* or "abiding" denotes an inward, enduring personal communion. They point out this inward, personal communion is not only directed upward with Christ but horizontally with other believers. Emphasis is also placed on the permanent nature of this relational intimacy, which is why *menō* is often translated as "remain." See Walter F. Bauer, Wilbur Gingrich, and Frederick W. Danker, *A Greek-English Lexicon of the New Testament and Other Early Christian Literature*, 2nd ed. (Chicago: University of Chicago Press, 1958), 504.

[4]One of the main Hebrew words for knowing is *yada'*, which is often used to describe a deep experiential knowledge of a person. This word is also used to describe the most intimate relational knowledge between a man and a woman. See Francis Brown, Edward Robinson, S. R. Driver, and Charles A. Briggs, *The New Brown, Driver, Briggs, Gesenius Hebrew and English Lexicon: With an Appendix Containing the Biblical Aramaic* (Peabody, MA: Hendrickson, 1979), 394.

[5]Matt Maher, "Abide with Me," *Saints and Sinners* (Nashville: Essential Records, 2015).

[6]C. Austin Miles, "In the Garden," 1912.

[7]In their document titled "A Christian Vision for Flourishing Communities," the Oikonomia Network makes a strong case for the intrinsic and symbiotic relationship between virtuous persons and flourishing economies. "What kind of economy we have is based on what kind of people we are; in turn, what kind of people we are will be affected by what kind of economy we have" (http://oikonomianetwork.org/wp-content/uploads/2014/02/EWP-NewVersion.pdf, 7).

[8]Dallas Willard and Gary Black Jr., *The Divine Conspiracy Continued* (San Francisco: HarperOne, 2014), 119. I highly recommend Dallas Willard's refreshing and insightful thoughts in the chapter titled "Illuminating the Good Life." Dallas Willard challenges our impoverished, privatized understanding of the Spirit-filled life. He opens the windows of possibilities regarding the influence and impact of Spirit-filled believers and Spirit-filled local church communities on the common good of society.

[9]The two Hebrew imperatives in Genesis 17:1, translated "walk before me" and "be blameless," speak of the restored intimacy of relationship and integrity of character now available to Abram as a grace gift from God. The intimacy and integrity once lost in the Garden of Eden will be restored in the Abrahamic Covenant, yet this too anticipates Christ's work on the cross for its ultimate fulfillment. In a sense, Genesis 17 both looks backward to the Garden and forward to the cross.

[10]Abraham's fruitful life of procreativity and productivity, which fulfills the cultural mandate of Genesis 1:28, is described in Genesis 17:2-8. There, the Genesis author points to future nations and kings that will come from Abraham, as well as the productivity of the good land of Canaan that will be Abraham's everlasting possession. It is important to note that the fruitfulness of Abraham's life in terms of material wealth and productivity is highlighted in Genesis 24:1-35.

[11] J. I. Packer, *A Man for All Ministries: Richard Baxter 1615-1691* (London: J. I. Packer, 1991), 4.

[12] Richard Baxter, *The Practical Works of Rev. Richard Baxter* (London: Richard Edwards, 1825), 122.

[13] Gene Veith, *God at Work: Your Christian Vocation in All of Life* (Wheaton, IL: Crossway, 2011), 7.

[14] For more on Scripture's affirmation of productivity and wealth see John R. Schneider, *The Good of Affluence: Seeking God in a Culture of Wealth* (Grand Rapids: Eerdmans, 2002).

5 LOVING THE NEIGHBORHOOD

[1] The Hebrew word *'ăbōdâ*, which is translated in Genesis 2:15 as "cultivate," is rendered in various ways throughout the Old Testament. In some contexts it is translated as "work," in others it is rendered as "service," and it is also used to denote "worship." It is used of farmers in Proverbs 12:11; textile workers in Isaiah 19:9, and priests in Numbers 3:7-8. In God's original creation design, work and worship were seamless. There was no Sunday-to-Monday gap. See Tom Nelson, *Work Matters: Connecting Sunday Worship to Monday Work* (Wheaton, IL: Crossway, 2011), 26-27. See also David Miller, *God at Work: The History and Promise of the Faith at Work Movement* (Oxford: Oxford University Press, 2007).

[2] The Hebrew word *'ēzer*, which is translated in Genesis 2:18 as "helper," appears throughout the Old Testament, most frequently with God as its subject. In Genesis 49:25, God is described as one who *helps* his people, blessing them abundantly. Moses declares God to be the *helper* who saved him from Pharaoh in Exodus 18:4. And the psalmist declares that he lifts his eyes up to the hills looking for *help* and finds that his "help comes from the LORD" in Psalm 121:1-2. The word also appears with reference to human subjects, often in military contexts, as in Joshua 1:14 and 2 Samuel 21:17. In this way, *'ēzer* speaks of mutual encouragement and cooperation that occurs when the strength of one is insufficient. See Willem VanGemeren, *New International Dictionary of Old Testament Theology and Exegesis* (Grand Rapids: Zondervan, 1997), 872-73.

[3] See Walter F. Bauer, Wilbur Gingrich, and Frederick W. Danker, *A Greek-English Lexicon of the New Testament and Other Early Christian Literature*, 2nd ed. (Chicago: University of Chicago Press, 1958), 697.

[4] Emmanuel Faber, "The World Needs Business Leadership with a Conscience," *Brewery* 1 (2014): 41.

[5]See James Davison Hunter, *To Change the World: The Irony, Tragedy, and Possibility of Christianity in the Late Modern World* (New York: Oxford University Press, 2010). Hunter describes both difference and dissolution as two authenticating marks of the late modern world, and calls Christians to embrace a cultural posture of faithful presence.

[6]See Brad Wilcox, "Marriage Is an Important Tool in the Fight Against Poverty," *FamilyStudies*, March 21, 2016, https://ifstudies.org/blog/marriage-is-an-important-tool-in-the-fight-against-poverty. See also W. Bradford Wilcox, "Family Structure Matters—Science Proves It," *National Review*, October 23, 2015, www.nationalreview.com/article/425957/family-structure-matters-w-bradford-wilcox. Also see http://heritage.org/research/reports/2010/09/marriage-america-s-greatest-weapon-against-child-poverty; and Kay S. Hymowitz, *Marriage and Caste in America: Separate and Unequal Families in a Post-Marital Age* (Chicago, IL: Ivan R Dee, 2007).

[7]Jay Steinmetz, "My Baltimore Business Problem," *Wall Street Journal*, May 4, 2015, A15.

[8]Thomas Sowell, *Basic Economics: A Common Sense Guide to the Economy* (New York: Basic Books, 2011), 5.

[9]See Wayne Grudem and Barry Asmus, *The Poverty of Nations: A Sustainable Solution* (Wheaton, IL: Crossway, 2013).

[10]Scott Rae, "Made for Responsibility," in *The Pastor's Guide to Fruitful Work and Economic Wisdom* (Overland Park, KS: Made to Flourish, 2012), 106-7.

[11]Raj Chetty's work is featured in Bob Davis, "Economist's Ideas Draw Interest on Both Sides of Aisle," *Wall Street Journal*, October 21, 2015.

[12]In her excellent book *Kingdom Calling*, Amy Sherman makes the case for the importance of vocational stewardship and gives examples of ways vocational stewardship is realized in our broader cultural context. See Amy Sherman, *Kingdom Calling: Vocational Stewardship for the Common Good* (Downers Grove, IL: InterVarsity Press, 2011).

[13]For example, see Jim Collins, *Good to Great and the Social Sectors* (New York: Collins Business, 2006), 19.

[14]Bob Shock, personal email exchange with the author, October 15, 2015.

[15]This argument is often associated with Milton Freidman, but there is a lot of debate as to whether he actually held this view. With the abuses of complex subprime mortgage investments offered by Wall Street and its damaging effects in the Great Recession, there have been increasing calls

for a more responsible multiple bottom-line approach to free-market economics. See Steven Garber, "The Economics of Mutuality, and More," *Faith, Vocation, and Culture*, May 26, 2013, www.washingtoninst.org/4834/the-economics-of-mutuality-and-more.

[16]Stephen M. Badger II, editorial in *The Brewery* 1 (2014): 2.

[17]I am also encouraged by the Mars Corporation's proactivity in supply chain management. For more, see "Responsible Sourcing: Supply Chain Transparency," *Mars*, accessed February 14, 2017, www.mars.com/global/sustainability/sustainable-sourcing-plan/responsible-sourcing.

6 ECONOMIC WISDOM

[1]For many years in my own pastoral ministry, I neglected economic reflection and engagement. See Tom Nelson, "Who's Serving Whom?," *Leadership Journal*, spring 2014.

[2]David Gill, "A Christian Vision for Flourishing Communities," *Oikonomia Network*, May 2016, 5, http://oikonomianetwork.org/wp-content/uploads/2016/07/Christian-Vision-for-Flourishing-Communities.pdf.

[3]While some critical scholars refute Solomon's authorship of Proverbs because the book bears similarities to other ancient collections of wisdom, there are many reasons to affirm that Israel's wise king assembled, adapted, and edited the book. First, Proverbs opens with a superscript that identifies Solomon as its principal author. Second, numerous citations within the book affirm Solomon's authorship (e.g., Prov 25:1). Third, Solomon's wisdom was well known in the ancient world. It is fair to assume that a ruler renown for his wisdom would be familiar with collections of wise sayings from neighboring cultures and might borrow sayings and structures from those collections. In other words, the similarities between Proverbs and other ancient writings do not disprove Solomon's authorship. Finally, the collections attributed to Solomon bear linguistic characteristics indicative of his time. All evidence considered, there is much reason to believe that Solomon indeed presided over the composition of Proverbs.

[4]John Bolt, *Economic Shalom: A Reformed Primer on Faith, Work, and Human Flourishing* (Grand Rapids: Christian's Library Press, 2013), 20.

[5]Thomas Sowell, *Basic Economics: A Citizen's Guide to the Economy* (New York: Basic Books, 2001), 429.

[6]For further elaboration on how work is embedded in a Christian anthropology, see Tom Nelson, *Work Matters* (Wheaton, IL: Crossway, 2011), chap. 1.

[7]The proverbs should not be understood as presenting absolute promises. Rather, they give general maxims. Many people in the world who work hard day after day remain quite impoverished. In other words, while diligence in work often leads to prosperity, this is not always the case. However, it is usually the case that prosperity remains illusive where diligence is lacking.

[8]In a *Wall Street Journal* article Lisa Ward writes, "The research, recently published in the *Journal of Economic Psychology*, found that donating to charity may actually improve a giver's physical and emotional well being. The study also suggested a link between increases in charitable tax subsidies, which have been found to spur giving, and improvements in people's perceptions of their own health. (Perception of health tends to be a good indicator of future health-care use and mortality rates.)" Lisa Ward, "Does Charitable Giving Lead to Better Health?," *Wall Street Journal*, February 1, 2015, www .wsj.com/articles/does-charitable-giving-lead-to-better-health-a-study -finds-a-link-1422849618. See also Christian Smith, *The Paradox of Generosity* (New York: Oxford University Press, 2014), which supports the goodness of generosity through quantitative data.

[9]Jesus' teaching in the Sermon on the Mount puts things in perspective when it comes to human life in an economic world. See Matthew 6:19-34.

7 WISDOM AND THE MODERN ECONOMY

[1]Robert A. Sirico, "The Moral Basis for Economic Liberty," *First Principles* 30 (Washington, DC: The Heritage Foundation, 2010), 2. See also Wayne Grudem and Barry Asmus, *The Poverty of Nations: A Sustainable Solution* (Wheaton, IL: Crossway, 2013), 142-43.

[2]For greater elaboration, see Barry Asmus and Wayne Grudem, "Property Rights Inherent in the Eighth Commandment Are Essential for Human Flourishing," in *Business Ethics Today*, ed. Philip J. Clements (Philadelphia: Center for Christian Business Ethics Today, 2011), 119-34.

[3]For more elaboration on why capital is in an economic system, how it works, and why it is so important for the vibrancy and velocity of an economy, I recommend reading chapter 3 of Hernando de Soto, *The Mystery of Capital: Why Capitalism Triumphs in the West and Fails Everywhere Else* (New York: Basic Books, 2000).

[4]Well-defined and consistently enforced property rights are a bedrock protection for the poor and vulnerable in a society. Many of the great injustices in history, such as Mao's Great Leap Forward, Pol Pot's Cambodian Killing

Fields, Stalin's purges through enforced famines, and the Nazi Holocaust, embody massive violations of property rights, particularly the right to self. Property rights not only expand opportunity but also provide protection from the powerful and vicious who will gladly abuse others.

[5]See David Kotter, "Greed vs. Self-Interest: A Case Study of How Economists Can Help Theologians Serve the Church," *Southern Baptist Journal of Theology* 19, no. 2 (2015): 17-47.

[6]John Bolt does a masterful work examining the influential work of Adam Smith and clarifying the difference between proper self-interest and selfishness. See John Bolt, *Economic Shalom: A Reformed Primer on Faith, Work, and Human Flourishing* (Grand Rapids: Christian's Library Press, 2013), 110-13.

[7]Steven E. Landsburg, *The Armchair Economist, Economics & Everyday Life* (New York: Free Press, 1995), 3.

[8]James D. Gwartney, Richard L. Stroup, Dwight R. Lee, and Tawni H. Ferrarini, *Common Sense Economics: What Everyone Should Know About Wealth and Prosperity* (New York: St. Martin's Press, 2010), 13.

[9]For example, the Moabite Ruth is provided opportunity by Boaz to glean in his fields. In this circumstance, Ruth was given a hand up, not a hand out (see Ruth 2:16-23). See also the prescriptive laws regarding gleaning in Leviticus 19:9-10.

[10]Governments should also not be an obstacle for ease of marketplace entry. Perhaps the most damaging monopolies are those that use governmental power to restrict entry. For example, occupational licensing has risen in the United States. While licensing does work to protect consumers, it also can be an undue burden for entry. Hair braiding, for example, is a way many African American women earn a living. However, licensing rules can require up to 2,100 hours of cosmetology training to get a license. See "Braiding," Institute for Justice, accessed February 15, 2017, http://ij.org/issues/economic -liberty/braiding.

[11]Thomas Sowell, *Basic Economics: A Citizen's Guide to the Economy* (New York: Basic Books, 2001), 179.

[12]De Soto, *Mystery of Capital*, 44.

[13]I am indebted to my friend P. J. Hill, who has consistently supported and encouraged me, patiently helping me navigate the complexities of modern economies. Dr. Hill's "trading game" illustration comes from a presentation he gave on June 10, 2016, titled "Economics for Pastors, Seven Economic Principles," Acton Institute, Grand Rapids, Michigan. For a short video

presentation that explains the gains of wealth from trade, see www .mruniversity.com/courses/principles-economics-microeconomics/trade -specialization-economics-globalization.

[14]Dallas Willard and Gary Black Jr., *The Divine Conspiracy Continued: Fulfilling God's Kingdom on Earth* (San Francisco: Harper One, 2014), 203.

[15]Leonard Read, "I, Pencil," Foundation for Economic Education, 1999, https://fee.org/resources/i-pencil-audio-pdf-and-html.

[16]Victor V. Claar and Robin K. Klay, *Economics in Christian Perspective: Theory, Policy and Life Choices* (Downers Grove, IL: IVP Academic, 2007), 168.

[17]In *Common Sense Economics,* the authors point to seven areas where government encourages a vital economy: (1) a consistent and fair legal system that protects private property rights and uniformly enforces contracts; (2) competitive markets that promote efficiency and innovation; (3) government regulations that are not onerous and unduly burdensome; (4) an efficient capital market that makes possible wealth creation activity; (5) monetary stability that makes possible exchange planning, predictability, and overall economic stability; (6) tax rates that do not stifle economic incentives for risk taking and rewards that come with value creation; (7) trade policies that minimize barriers and encourage opportunities to buy and sell goods locally and globally. See Gwartney, Stroup, Lee, and Ferrarini, *Common Sense Economics*, 4.

[18]To read more about Paige Chenault as well as other women who use their business acumen for the good of their neighbors, visit "Women to Watch," *Grit & Virtue*, accessed February 15, 2017, https://gritandvirtue.com /women-to-watch.

8 WISE GENEROSITY

[1]Veronica Dagher, "The Rich Get Richer as Billionaires Increase in Number," *Wall Street Journal,* August 8, 2016, www.wsj.com/articles/the-rich-get -richer-as-billionaires-increase-in-number-1470628860.

[2]The *Wall Street Journal* reports, "The world's billionaire population grew by 6.4% to 2,473 in 2015. Billionaires controlled 3.9% of the world's total household wealth in 2015, slightly down from 4% in 2014, according to Wealth-X, a consulting group that uses public records and research staff to manually track the habits of ultra-high-net-worth individuals, or people valued at more than $30 million" (ibid.).

[3]Encouraging examples of a revolution in generosity include the Generous

Giving Conferences, as well as books like Wesley K. Willmer, *Revolution in Generosity: Transforming Stewards to Be Rich Toward God* (Chicago: Moody Publishers, 2008); Kenneth H. Blanchard and S. Truett Cathy, *The Generosity Factor: Discover the Joy of Giving Your Time, Talent, and Treasure* (Grand Rapids: Zondervan, 2002); National Christian Foundation, *Generosity: Moving Toward Life That Is Truly Life* (Alpharetta, GA: National Christian Foundation, 2009); William F. High and Ashley B. McCauley, *The Generosity Bet: Secrets of Risk, Reward, and Real Joy* (Shippensburg, PA: Destiny Image, 2014); and Ron Blue and Jodie Berndt, *Generous Living: Finding Contentment Through Giving* (Grand Rapids: Zondervan, 1997).

[4]Any reflection on financial stewardship presupposes other stewardships that influence overall directional priorities and specific decision grids. For example, knowledge stewardship must be taken seriously as we manage and curate information God makes available to us through a variety of epistemological conduits. The apostle Paul reminds us that as followers of Christ we are "servants of Christ and stewards of the mysteries of God" (1 Cor 4:1).

[5]Harold Best says, "God is the uniquely Continuous Outpourer. He cannot but give of himself, reveal himself, pour himself out. Even before he chooses to create, and before he chooses to reveal himself beyond himself, he eternally pours himself out to his triune Self in unending fellowship, ceaseless conversation and immeasurable love unto an infinity of the same." Harold Best, *Unceasing Worship: Biblical Perspectives on Worship and the Arts* (Downers Grove, IL: InterVarsity Press, 2003), 20.

[6]Ibid., 23.

[7]Randy C. Alcorn, *Money, Possessions, and Eternity* (Wheaton, IL: Tyndale House Publishers, 2003), 172, 184.

[8]We see this priority in giving at the early dawn of creation, when Cain and Abel bring offerings to God from the first fruits of their work. For some reason, most likely a wrongfully motivated heart, Cain's first fruits giving was rejected by God.

[9]In Matthew 6:21, Jesus says, "Where your treasure is, there your heart will be also." The order is important to grasp. Our heart follows in lock step what we truly treasure.

[10]John R. Schneider, *The Good of Affluence: Seeking God in a Culture of Wealth* (Grand Rapids: Eerdmans, 2002), 165. Schneider astutely observes, "The way into the kingdom for Zaccheus was not poverty, or even withdrawal

from his home and line of work. Salvation comes to his house through creative and redemptive uses of his economic power" (ibid., 187).

[11]There is a significant degree of debate about tithing both in the Old Testament and in the New Testament. Some see discontinuity, while others see continuity. In my opinion, Randy Alcorn rightly sees a strong thread of continuity, concluding that Jesus didn't ever suggest "the floor set by the tithe was eliminated, but rather that the ceiling of Christian giving was far above it." See Alcorn, *Money, Possessions, and Eternity*, 216. Craig Blomberg takes a more discontinuous view, making the case that the Old Testament tithing was actually more than 10 percent but actually something closer to 23 percent. He also dismisses New Testament tithing: "In the New Testament age, no specific percentage is commanded of believers." I do not find Blomberg's argument convincing. See Craig L. Blomberg, "God and Money: A Biblical Theology of Possessions," in *Revolution in Generosity*, ed. Wesley K. Willmer (Chicago: Moody Publishers, 2008), 53.

[12]The primacy of the local church in both God's desire and design is overwhelmingly seen throughout the New Testament. Theologian Miroslav Volf makes this important point when he says that the word for church (*ekklēsia*) in the New Testament "refers almost exclusively to the concrete assembly of Christians at a specific place." See Miroslav Volf, *After Our Likeness: The Church as the Image of the Trinity* (Grand Rapids: Eerdmans, 1998), 137. For further elaboration of this key point, see author's booklet *Giving God Our Best*, 17-20.

[13]Craig Van Gelder insightfully makes a compelling case for the primacy of the local visible church in New Testament ecclesiology: "The authors of the New Testament did not distinguish between the visible and the invisible church. To them, the church that existed in the world was the only church there was" (Craig Van Gelder, *The Essence of the Church: A Community Created by the Spirit* [Grand Rapids: Baker, 2000], 105). Van Gelder continues, "But we do an injustice to the teaching of the New Testament authors if we impose this conception of the invisible church on the ideas they formulated. These authors were describing the concrete, historical, visible church that had come into existence in their day, and which was rapidly spreading throughout the Mediterranean world. It is this church that they chose to label the ecclesia" (ibid., 106). Van Gelder also makes the important connection of the local church to the gospel: "The biblical story is contextualized in the life of the church. The church becomes, in fact, the

hermeneutic of the gospel. That is the world is able to understand the truthfulness of the gospel story by reading the story of the life of the church" (ibid., 144). See Van Gelder, *Essence of the Church*.

[14] I am indebted to James Davison Hunter's excellent formulation of the call of the church to be a faithful presence within its cultural context. I recommend Hunter's insightful book addressing this topic: James Davison Hunter, *To Change the World: The Irony, Tragedy, and Possibility of Christianity in the Late Modern World* (New York: Oxford University Press, 2010).

[15] Alcorn, *Money, Possessions, and Eternity*, 214. I recommend chapter 12, titled "Tithing: The First Step of Giving."

[16] Craig Van Gelder asserts this stunning vision of the church as he points to Jesus' prayer in Matthew 6. See Van Gelder, *Essence of the Church*, 43.

[17] Philip Yancey, *Church, Why Bother? My Personal Pilgrimage* (Grand Rapids: Zondervan, 1998), 23.

[18] R. Scott Rodin, "The Transformation of the Godly Steward," in *Revolution in Generosity*, ed. Wesley K. Willmer (Chicago, IL: Moody Publishers, 2008), 117.

[19] Ben Patterson, quoted in Richard J. Towner, "The Church's Leadership Role in Bringing Stewardship Front and Center," in Willmer, *Revolution in Generosity*, 121.

[20] For a broader discussion of the local church and particularly the importance of the bride of Christ metaphor, see Tom Nelson, *Ekklesia: Rediscovering God's Design for the Church* (Kearney, NE: Cross Training, 2010).

[21] Alcorn, *Money, Possessions, and Eternity*, 130.

9 THE POOR AMONG US

[1] "For the first time in U.S. history, more poor people live in suburbs than in cities" (Steve Corbett and Brian Fikkert, *When Helping Hurts: How to Alleviate Poverty Without Hurting the Poor and Yourself* [Chicago: Moody Publishers, 2009], 183). "One of the tricky features of the new suburban poverty is that it is less visible than traditional, inner city poverty" (ibid., 184).

[2] Ibid., 62.

[3] Mother Teresa, *Mother Teresa: Her Essential Wisdom*, ed. Carol Kelly-Gangi (New York: Barnes & Noble, 2006), 32.

[4] Corbett and Fikkert, *When Helping Hurts*, 53.

[5]N. T. Wright, *Evil and the Justice of God* (Downers Grove, IL: InterVarsity Press, 2006), 25.

[6]Jesus offered chilling and sobering words when he asked, "What will it profit a man if he gains the whole world and forfeits his soul?" (Mt 16:26).

[7]Scott B. Rae, *Introducing Christian Ethics: A Short Guide to Making Moral Choices* (Grand Rapids: Zondervan, 2016), 160.

[8]While the importance of this parable should not be minimized in any way, neither should it be interpreted to the exclusion of Jesus' other teaching and parables on material wealth. I applaud much about economic curriculums like "Lazarus at the Gate" and the good work being done by the Boston Faith & Justice Network (bostonfaithjustice.org). However, caring for the global poor and addressing global poverty will take more than simpler living and generous giving; it will also take an emphasis on economic capacity building and job creation throughout the world.

[9]Kenneth C. Bailey, *Jesus Through Middle Eastern Eyes: Cultural Studies in the Gospels* (Downers Grove, IL: IVP Academic, 2008), 395.

[10]See also 2 Corinthians 8–9, where Paul makes a financial appeal and affirms the integrity of the mission to the poor.

[11]Corbett and Fikkert, *When Helping Hurts*, 65.

[12]Corbett and Fikkert write, "We are not bringing Christ to poor communities. He has been active in these communities since the creation of the world, 'sustaining them by his powerful word' (Heb. 1:3). Hence, a significant part of working in poor communities involves discovering and appreciating what God has been doing there for a long time! This should give us a sense of humility and awe as we enter poor communities, for part of what we see there reflects the very hand of God" (ibid., 60).

[13]Timothy Keller, *Generous Justice: How God's Grace Makes Us Just* (New York: Penguin Books, 2010), 34.

[14]For greater elaboration, see Robert Lupton's excellent book *Toxic Charity: How Churches and Charities Hurt Those They Help (and How to Reverse It)* (New York: HarperOne, 2011), which identifies ways that modern charitable enterprises harm those they intend to help, and introduces more effective methods for assisting the vulnerable.

[15]Corbett and Fikkert, *When Helping Hurts*, 131.

[16]Andy Crouch, *Playing God, Redeeming the Gift of Power* (Downers Grove, IL: InterVarsity Press, 2013), 150.

[17]J. D. Vance's *Hillbilly Elegy* is an acclaimed book that gives fascinating insight into the life of the rural poor. J. D. Vance, *Hillbilly Elegy: A Memoir of a Family and Culture in Crisis* (New York: Harper, 2016).

10 ECONOMIC INJUSTICE

[1]Note particularly the emphasis on honest scales in commercial transactions in order not to defraud or take advantage of the foreigner (Lev 19:35-36).

[2]See Nicholas Wolterstorff, *Until Justice and Peace Embrace* (Grand Rapids: Eerdmans, 1983). Wolterstorff makes the point that the deeper reason informing why we should care for and defend the poor is that we are called to uphold their rights and dignity as fellow image bearers of God. If we do not defend the poor, Wolterstorff contends, we are violating the God-given rights of poor persons. Wolterstorff calls the church to engage in matters of justice, highlighting four basic rights of the poor that are often abused and need to be addressed: (1) rights of protection, (2) rights of freedom, (3) rights to voice or participation, and (4) rights to sustenance.

[3]Amos describes the economic injustice perpetrated toward the economically vulnerable as "dealing deceitfully with false balances" and deceptively "selling the chaff of the wheat" (Amos 8:5-6).

[4]Some have suggested that moving away from a free-market economic system toward a more socialist system might diminish profit motive and thereby increase economic justice and welfare for the poor. Randy Alcorn offers a thoughtful response: "Those who laud socialism as an alternative to capitalism ignore the fact that historically the poor usually fare better in capitalistic economies than socialist ones. Furthermore they fail to recognize that when the incentive of individual profit for labor is removed, because no one is allowed to get ahead, then someone must find a way to motivate people to work. There is just one other way—coercion. Capitalism says, 'You scratch my back and I'll scratch yours.' Socialism says, 'You scratch my back or I'll break yours.' Can capitalism lead to exploitation of the poor? Of course. Does socialism usually lead to oppression of the poor? Yes. The point is not that capitalism is so good, but that the alternatives are so bad. It isn't a system problem, but a sin problem. Any economic system will work where there is no sin. None will work ideally when there is sin. But some may work better than others." Randy Alcorn, *Money, Possessions, and Eternity* (Wheaton, IL: Tyndale House, 2003), 248.

[5] Andy Crouch, *Playing God: Redeeming the Gift of Power* (Downers Grove, IL: InterVarsity Press, 2013), 83.

[6] Bethany McLean, "Payday Lending: Will Anything Better Replace It?," *Atlantic*, May 2016, www.theatlantic.com/magazine/archive/2016/05 /payday-lending/476403.

[7] Ibid.

[8] See Derek Thompson, "Lotteries: America's $70 Billion Shame," *Atlantic*, May 11, 2015, www.theatlantic.com/business/archive/2015/05/lotteries -americas-70-billion-shame/392870.

[9] See Kevin Fox Gotham, *Race, Real Estate, and Uneven Development: The Kansas City Experience, 1900-2010* (Albany: State University of New York Press, 2002).

[10] See Michael O. Emerson and Christian Smith, *Divided by Faith: Evangelical Religion and Race in America* (New York: Oxford University Press, 2001).

[11] N. T. Wright speaks with great insight here: "God's justice is not simply a blind dispensing of rewards for the virtuous and punishments for the wicked, though plenty of those are to be found on the way. God's justice is a saving, healing, restorative justice, because the God to whom justice belongs is the Creator God who has yet to complete his original plan for creation and whose justice is designed not simply to restore balance to a world out of kilter but to bring to glorious completion and fruition the creation, teeming with life and possibility, that he made in the first place." N. T. Wright, *Evil and the Justice of God* (Downers Grove, IL: InterVarsity Press, 2006), 64.

[12] Tim Keller, *Generous Justice* (New York: Penguin Books, 2010), 130.

[13] One helpful way to grow in humble understanding and empathy is to engage thoughtful literature. Recent books that engage racial discrimination and open the window to the tragedy of prejudice and injustice include Ta-Nehisi Coates, *Between the World and Me* (New York: Spiegel & Grau, 2015); and Matthew Desmond, *Evicted: Poverty and Profit in the American City* (New York: Crown, 2016).

[14] Christ Community Church has and continues to partner with Christian Fellowship Baptist Church in multiple ways to advance Christ's kingdom agenda in the Kansas City metro area. As equals, committed to the gospel and to a mission of reconciliation together, we have learned and continue to learn from each other how to love one another in hard places of our brokenness.

[15] D. A. Carson, *Love in Hard Places* (Wheaton, IL: Crossway, 2002), 101.

[16]Crouch, *Playing God*, 19.

[17]Steve Corbett and Brian Fikkert, *When Helping Hurts: How to Alleviate Poverty Without Hurting the Poor and Yourself* (Chicago: Moody Publishers, 2009), 142.

[18]Rick Warren, quoted in Wayne Grudem and Barry Asmus, *The Poverty of Nations* (Wheaton, IL: Crossway, 2013), 20.

[19]See Gary Haugen and Victor Boutros, *The Locust Effect: Why the End of Poverty Requires the End of Violence* (New York: Oxford University Press, 2014).

[20]Theologian Wayne Grudem and economist Barry Asmus make a strong case for the importance of the free market as a vital factor in moving poorer nations to greater economic prosperity. However, they rightly point out the free market itself is not a magic bullet for poverty alleviation. See Grudem and Asmus, *Poverty of Nations*.

[21]Ibid., 309.

11 REBUILDING THE RUINS

[1]Miroslav Volf, *A Public Faith: How Followers of Christ Should Serve the Common Good* (Grand Rapids: Baker, 2011), 74.

[2]Steven Garber, *Visions of Vocation: Common Grace for the Common Good* (Downers Grove, IL: InterVarsity Press, 2014), 18. I recommend Steve's outstanding book. You will not only see the world with greater clarity, you will have greater wisdom and insight for knowing how God would have you personally respond.

[3]In his book *Jesus Through Middle Eastern Eyes*, Kenneth Bailey brilliantly captures the essence of Jesus' story through the final words of the vineyard owner, "You are free to do what you like with what is yours. And I am free to do what I like with what is mine. I chose to pay these men a living wage. You will be able to go home to your wives and children and proudly announce that you found work and have a full day's pay. I want these other men to be able to walk in the doors of their houses with the same joy in their hearts and the same money in their pockets. I want their children to be as proud of them as yours are of you. So you worked through the heat of the day did you? That's fine. And what do you think I was doing during the heat of the day? Enjoying a traditional siesta? I was on the road to and from the market—trying to demonstrate compassion to others who like you, are in need of employment. I could have sent my manager to do this. I didn't. I went myself to demonstrate solidarity with the men and help

alleviate their suffering. Why are you jealous of them and angry at me? You must understand that I am not only just—I am also merciful and compassionate, because mercy and compassion are a part of justice." Kenneth Bailey, *Jesus Through Middle Eastern Eyes* (Downers Grove, IL: IVP Academic, 2008), 361.

[4]See Thomas Friedman, *The World Is Flat* (New York: Farrar, Straus & Giroux, 2005).

[5]Andy Crouch, *Playing God* (Downers Grove, IL: InterVarsity Press, 2013), 84.

[6]Tim Keller, *Center Church: Doing Balanced, Gospel-Centered Ministry in Your City* (Grand Rapids: Zondervan, 2012), 371. Particularly insightful is chapter 30, "The City and the Gospel Ecosystem." In addition to vibrant church-planting efforts across denominational lines, Keller points to seven "third ring" components: (1) a prayer movement, (2) a number of specialized evangelistic ministries, (3) an array of justice and mercy ministries, (4) faith and work initiatives, (5) institutions supporting family life, schools, and counseling services, (6) systems for attracting and developing urban church leaders, and (7) the unity of Christian city leaders.

[7]Richard J. Goossen and R. Paul Stevens, *Entrepreneurial Leadership: Finding Your Calling, Making a Difference* (Downers Grove, IL: InterVarsity Press, 2013), 68.

[8]Victor V. Claar and Robin J. Klay, *Economics in Christian Perspective* (Downers Grove, IL: IVP Academic, 2007), 214.

[9]See Tim Keller, *Preaching: Communicating Faith in an Age of Skepticism* (New York: Viking, 2015).

[10]Bill Peel and Walt Larimore, *Workplace Grace: Becoming a Spiritual Influence at Work* (Longview, TX: LeTourneau Press, 2014), 19. I recommend this book both for its theological depth as well as its practical guidance in equipping followers of Jesus to share the most glorious and transforming news with their coworkers.

[11]Ibid., 28.

[12]In his letter to the Romans, Paul connects the logical dots of the necessity of gospel proclamation: "How then will they call on him in whom they have not believed? And how are they to believe in him of whom they have never heard? And how are they to hear without someone preaching?" Paul then concludes, "So faith comes from hearing, and hearing through the word of Christ" (Rom 10:14, 17).

12 GETTING TO WORK

[1]Peter Drucker, quoted in Richard J. Goossen and R. Paul Stevens, *Entrepreneurial Leadership: Finding Your Calling, Making a Difference* (Downers Grove, IL: InterVarsity Press, 2013), 22.

[2]I recommend Goossen and Steven's book *Entrepreneurial Leadership*. The authors point out five tenets of entrepreneurial leaders: (1) innovation, (2) seizing opportunities, (3) gaining personal satisfaction through innovation, (4) doing risk analysis, and (5) developing entrepreneurial habits. Goossen and Stevens, *Entrepreneurial Leadership*, 23-28.

[3]The Kauffman Foundation (kauffman.org) is a national leader in fostering entrepreneurship among a diverse constituency aimed at the flourishing of cities. Presently, 1 Million Cups (1millioncups.com) attracts an estimated national weekly attendance of more than twenty-five hundred people.

[4]See Renew Counseling Center's website, www.renewkc.com. Kori Bohn, the entrepreneurial founder of Renew Counseling Center, tells her story in Tom Nelson, *Work Matters: Connecting Sunday Worship to Monday Work* (Wheaton, IL: Crossway, 2011), 202-3.

[5]Magatte Wade, quoted in "Another Successful Acton University Has Come and Gone," *Acton Institute Newsletter* 26, no. 4 (July-August 2016).

[6]Peter Greer and Chris Horst, *Entrepreneurship for Human Flourishing* (Washington, DC: American Enterprise Institute for Public Policy Research, 2014), 22.

[7]Ibid., 6.

[8]Robert Lupton, interview by Bethany Hoang, "How to Help Those in Need (Without Treating Them Like Beggars)," *Christianity Today*, November 2015. I also highly recommend Robert Lupton's book *Charity Detox: What Charity Would Look Like If We Cared About Results* (New York: HarperOne, 2015).

[9]For example, Dave Ramsey's Financial Peace University has helped many congregants better manage the economic resources entrusted to them.

[10]Matt Perman, *What's Best Next: How the Gospel Transforms the Way You Get Things Done* (Grand Rapids: Zondervan, 2014), 66.

[11]Perman's *What's Best Next* has been a must read in the development of our local church staff. Matt also gave a hands-on, practical seminar to our church staff on ways to increase productivity in our work. We not only want to do the right things but to do the right things well. Ongoing productivity

training helps us move in that desired direction, with the ultimate goal of moving our mission forward and glorifying God.

[12]Tim Keller observes, "Any large-scale improvement in a society's level of poverty will come through a comprehensive array of public and private, spiritual, personal and corporate measures." Tim Keller, *Generous Justice* (New York: Penguin Books, 2012), 34.

[13]See Steve Corbett and Brian Fikkert, *When Helping Hurts: How to Alleviate Poverty Without Hurting the Poor and Yourself* (Chicago: Moody Publishers, 2009), esp. chap. 4.

[14]Christ Community Church has hosted two Common Good conferences (CG 2013 and CG 2015), where a diverse representation of business, education, arts, church, and government leaders have come together for a day of engagement around the common good of our city. We also partner closely with the Culture House (culturehouse.com), which is training a new generation of artists within our city.

[15]Corbett and Fikkert, *When Helping Hurts*, 189-90.

[16]While Nehemiah 1–6 record the rebuilding of the wall of Jerusalem, chapters 7-13 speak of the spiritual renewal of the people.

[17]See Nelson, *Work Matters*, chap. 10.

[18]Amy L. Sherman, *Kingdom Calling: Vocational Stewardship for the Common Good* (Downers Grove, IL: InterVarsity Press, 2011), 21.

[19]Ibid., 144-50. For more elaboration on this helpful rubric for vocational stewardship, see p. 22 and chapters 9-13 (pp. 143-222).

[20]See Richard Hays, *The Moral Vision of the New Testament* (New York: Harper One, 1996), 13. "The book of Acts gives no evidence of the apostles seeking to reform political structures outside the church either through protest or seizing power. Instead Luke tells the story of the formation of a new community—the church—in which goods are shared and wrongs are put to right. . . . The question that Luke-Acts puts to the church—then and now—is not 'Are you reforming society?' but rather 'Is the power of the resurrection at work among you?'" (ibid., 135).

[21]Charlie Self, *Flourishing Churches and Communities: A Pentecostal Primer on Faith, Work, and Economics for Spirit-Empowered Discipleship* (Grand Rapids: Christian's Library Press, 2013), 66.

13 THE HOPE OF THE WORLD

[1]John Stott, *The Living Church: Convictions of a Lifelong Pastor* (Downers Grove, IL: InterVarsity Press, 2007), 19.

[2]Simon Sinek, *Start with Why: How Great Leaders Inspire Everyone to Take Action* (New York: Portfolio, 2009), 39.

[3]Jim Clifton, *The Coming Jobs War* (New York: Gallup Press, 2011), 10.

[4]Steven Garber, *Visions of Vocation: Common Grace for the Common Good* (Downers Grove, IL: InterVarsity Press, 2014), 135.

Will you join with us today?

Apply for the network at madetoflourish.org/apply.

For more written, video, and audio resources, visit us at madeto flourish.org. You can also stay in touch by following us on Twitter (@madetoflourish) and liking us on Facebook (facebook.com/ MTFpastor).

Made to Flourish
10901 Lowell Ave, Ste 130
Overland Park, KS 66210
info@madetoflourish.org | madetoflourish.org

MADE TO FLOURISH
A PASTORS' NETWORK FOR THE COMMON GOOD

The pastoral work you are called to do plays an important role in nurturing human flourishing and furthering the common good. We want to be a helpful resource as you faithfully equip your congregation to be followers of Jesus in all dimensions of life.

That's why we exist. Made to Flourish is a nationwide membership organization that equips pastors with a deeper understanding of the essential connection between Sunday faith and Monday work. Our goal is to help empower you to lead flourishing churches. As congregants begin to understand the intrinsic value of their daily work to God, it completely transforms their perspective on their work and how they do it.

Membership is free—we exist solely to provide you with relationships and resources to strengthen your ministry. We do this through a monthly newsletter, a resource-filled website, national events, online workshops and webinars, and city networks where you can meet with other local pastors.

By becoming a member, you will receive a welcome kit with several core faith-and-work resources, be connected to a city network, and receive special access to our events, seminars, and online learning opportunities.

WILL YOU JOIN WITH US TODAY?

Apply for the network at **madetoflourish.org/apply**.

For more written, video, and audio resources,
visit us at **madetoflourish.org**. You can also stay in touch by
following us on Twitter (**@madetoflourish**) and liking us on
Facebook (**facebook.com/MTFpastor**).

MADE TO FLOURISH

10901 Lowell Ave, Ste 130 | Overland Park, KS 66210
info@madetoflourish.org | www.madetoflourish.org